William Shakespeare's

Henry IV: Part One
In Plain and Simple English

BookCaps Study Guides
www.bookcaps.com

Table of Contents:

About This Series

The "Classic Retold" series started as a way of telling classics for the modern reader—being careful to preserve the themes and integrity of the original. Whether you want to understand Shakespeare a little more or are trying to get a better grasps of the Greek classics, there is a book waiting for you!

Characters

King Henry the Fourth.

Henry, Prince of Wales, son to the King.

Prince John of Lancaster, son to the King.

Earl of Westmoreland.

Sir Walter Blunt.

Thomas Percy, Earl of Worcester.

Henry Percy, Earl of Northumberland.

Henry Percy, surnamed Hotspur, his son.

Edmund Mortimer, Earl of March.

Richard Scroop, Archbishop of York.

Archibald, Earl of Douglas.

Owen Glendower.

Sir Richard Vernon.

Sir John Falstaff.

Sir Michael, a friend to the Archbishop of York.

Poins.

Gadshill

Peto.

Bardolph.

Lady Percy, wife to Hotspur, and sister to Mortimer.

Lady Mortimer, daughter to Glendower, and wife to Mortimer.

Mistress Quickly, hostess of the Boar's Head in Eastcheap.

Lords, Officers, Sheriff, Vintner, Chamberlain, Drawers, two

Carriers, Travellers, and Attendants.

SCENE.--England and Wales.

Act I

Scene I.

London. The Palace.

Enter the King, Lord John of Lancaster, Earl of Westmoreland,
[Sir Walter Blunt,] with others.

King.
So shaken as we are, so wan with care,
Find we a time for frighted peace to pant
And breathe short-winded accents of new broils
To be commenc'd in stronds afar remote.
No more the thirsty entrance of this soil
Shall daub her lips with her own children's blood.
No more shall trenching war channel her fields,
Nor Bruise her flow'rets with the armed hoofs
Of hostile paces. Those opposed eyes
Which, like the meteors of a troubled heaven,
All of one nature, of one substance bred,
Did lately meet in the intestine shock
And furious close of civil butchery,
Shall now in mutual well-beseeming ranks
March all one way and be no more oppos'd
Against acquaintance, kindred, and allies.
The edge of war, like an ill-sheathed knife,
No more shall cut his master. Therefore, friends,
As far as to the sepulchre of Christ-
Whose soldier now, under whose blessed cross
We are impressed and engag'd to fight-
Forthwith a power of English shall we levy,
Whose arms were moulded in their mother's womb
To chase these pagans in those holy fields
Over whose acres walk'd those blessed feet
Which fourteen hundred years ago were nail'd
For our advantage on the bitter cross.
But this our purpose now is twelvemonth old,
And bootless 'tis to tell you we will go.
Therefore we meet not now. Then let me hear
Of you, my gentle cousin Westmoreland,
What yesternight our Council did decree

In forwarding this dear expedience.

As shaken as we are, so pale with stress,
will find a time in all this chaos to catch our breath,
and, puffing, talk of new battles
to be begun in faraway lands:
no more shall the thirsty mouth of this soil
paint her lips with her own children's blood,
the trenches of war shall no longer score her fields,
and her flowers will no longer be bruised with the armoured hoofs
of enemy horses: those conflicting eyes,
which, like the meteors in a stormy sky,
are all the same, all bread from the same stock,
which recently met in the internal shock
and furious battles of civil war,
will now, in interdependent well ordered ranks,
all march together, and no longer confront
friends, family and allies.
The blade of wars will no longer cut his master
like a carelessly stowed knife. Therefore, friends,
we shall go to the tomb of Christ–
whose soldier we are now, under whose blessed cross
we are conscripted and bound to fight–
we shall raise an English force,
who were born to fight,
to chase these pagans in those holy fields
on which those blessed feet walked
which fourteen hundred years ago were nailed
on the bitter cross for our benefit.
But this plan of ours is now twelve months old,
and it's pointless to tell you we will go;
that's not why we are meeting now. So let me hear
from you, my gentle cousin Westmorland,
what our Council decided last night
to move on this cherished and urgent enterprise.

West.
My liege, this haste was hot in question
And many limits of the charge set down
But yesternight; when all athwart there came
A post from Wales, loaden with heavy news;
Whose worst was that the noble Mortimer,
Leading the men of Herefordshire to fight
Against the irregular and wild Glendower,

Was by the rude hands of that Welshman taken,
A thousand of his people butchered;
Upon whose dead corpse there was such misuse,
Such beastly shameless transformation,
By those Welshwomen done as may not be
Without much shame retold or spoken of.

My lord, this urgency was eagerly debated,
and many assignments had been handed out
just yesterday night, when all of a sudden there came
a messenger from Wales, carrying grim news,
the worst of which was that noble Mortimer,
leading the men of Herefordshire to fight
against the wild guerilla bands of Glendower,
was captured by the rough hands of that Welshman,
a thousand of his people were butchered,
whose dead bodies were so abused,
so brutally mutilated
by those Welsh women, that it can't be
spoken of without much shame.

King.
It seems then that the tidings of this broil
Brake off our business for the Holy Land.

So it seems that the news of this battle
means we must suspend our plans for the Holy Land.

West.
This, match'd with other, did, my gracious lord;
For more uneven and unwelcome news
Came from the North, and thus it did import:
On Holy-rood Day the gallant Hotspur there,
Young Harry Percy, and brave Archibald,
That ever-valiant and approved Scot,
At Holmedon met,
Where they did spend a sad and bloody hour;
As by discharge of their artillery
And shape of likelihood the news was told;
For he that brought them, in the very heat
And pride of their contention did take horse,
Uncertain of the issue any way.

This, coupled with something else, does, my gracious Lord,

10

for even more disturbing and unwelcome news
came from the North, telling us this:
on the day of the Holy Cross, gallant Hotspur there,
young Harry Percy, and brave Archibald,
that always courageous and renowned Scott,
met at Holmedon, where they clashed in
a sad and bloody battle;
we were told the news that we would lose
on the basis of the probable result
based on the way the battle went so far;
for the one who brought it had left
right in the very heat of battle,
so he was uncertain as to the outcome.

King.
Here is a dear, a true-industrious friend,
Sir Walter Blunt, new lighted from his horse,
Stain'd with the variation of each soil
Betwixt that Holmedon and this seat of ours,
And he hath brought us smooth and welcome news.
The Earl of Douglas is discomfited;
Ten thousand bold Scots, two-and-twenty knights,
Balk'd in their own blood did Sir Walter see
On Holmedon's plains. Of prisoners, Hotspur took
Mordake Earl of Fife and eldest son
To beaten Douglas, and the Earl of Athol,
Of Murray, Angus, and Menteith.
And is not this an honourable spoil?
A gallant prize? Ha, cousin, is it not?

Here is a dear loyal and zealous friend,
Sir Walter Blunt, newly dismounted from his horse,
stained with every type of soil
that exists between that Holmedon and our palace;
and he has brought us hopeful and welcome news.
The Earl of Douglas has been thwarted;
ten thousand bold Scotsmen, and twenty two knights,
choked with their own blood, Sir Walter saw
on the plains of Holmedon; Hotspur took
Mordrake, Earl of Fife and the oldest son
of beaten Douglas, and the Earl of Athol,
of Murray, Angus and Mentieth, prisoner:
isn't this an honourable haul?
A gallant prize? Ha, cousin, isn't it?

West.
In faith,
It is a conquest for a prince to boast of.

By God,
it is a triumph for a prince to boast of.

King.
Yea, there thou mak'st me sad, and mak'st me sin
In envy that my Lord Northumberland
Should be the father to so blest a son-
A son who is the theme of honour's tongue,
Amongst a grove the very straightest plant;
Who is sweet Fortune's minion and her pride;
Whilst I, by looking on the praise of him,
See riot and dishonour stain the brow
Of my young Harry. O that it could be prov'd
That some night-tripping fairy had exchang'd
In cradle clothes our children where they lay,
And call'd mine Percy, his Plantagenet!
Then would I have his Harry, and he mine.
But let him from my thoughts. What think you, coz,
Of this young Percy's pride? The prisoners
Which he in this adventure hath surpris'd
To his own use he keeps, and sends me word
I shall have none but Mordake Earl of Fife.

Well, saying that you make me sad, can make me sin
by envying my Lord Northumberland
for being the father of such a wonderful son;
a son who is the very soul of honour,
the very straightest tree in the forest,
who is the darling of fate and her joy;
when I look at people praising him
all I can see is the riotous behaviour and dishonour
which mars the appearance of my young Harry. Oh, if it could be proved
that some fairy in the night had exchanged
our children when they lay in their cots,
and called mine Percy, his Plantagenet!
Then I would have his Harry, and he mine:
but I won't think about him. What do you think, cousin,
of the arrogance of this young Percy? The prisoners
whom he has captured in this adventure

he is keeping for his own purposes, and he sends me word
that I shall have none except Mordrake, Earl of Fife.

West.

This is his uncle's teaching, this Worcester,
Malevolent to you In all aspects,
Which makes him prune himself and bristle up
The crest of youth against your dignity.

This is the teaching of his uncle, this Worcester,
who hates you in every respect,
this is what makes him puff himself up
and oppose your dignity with his youth.

King.

But I have sent for him to answer this;
And for this cause awhile we must neglect
Our holy purpose to Jerusalem.
Cousin, on Wednesday next our council we
Will hold at Windsor. So inform the lords;
But come yourself with speed to us again;
For more is to be said and to be done
Than out of anger can be uttered.

I have summonsed him to answer for this;
and because of this for a while we must
neglect our holy business in Jerusalem.
Cousin, next Wednesday we will hold a council
at Windsor. Inform the lords;
but afterwards hurry back to me;
I am so angry that there is more to be said and to be done
than we can speak of in public.

West.

I will my liege.

I will, my lord.

Exeunt.

Scene II. The same. An Apartment of Prince Henry's.

[Enter Prince Henry and Falstaff.]

FAL.
Now, Hal, what time of day is it, lad?

Now, Hal, what time of day is it, lad?

PRINCE.
Thou art so fat-witted, with drinking of old sack, and
unbuttoning thee after supper, and sleeping upon benches
after noon, that thou hast forgotten to demand that truly which
thou wouldst truly know. What a devil hast thou to do with the
time of the day? unless hours were cups of sack, and minutes
capons, and the blessed Sun himself a fair hot wench in
flame-coloured taffeta, I see no reason why thou shouldst be
so superfluous to demand the time of the day.

You've become so stupid by drinking Spanish wine
and slobbing out after supper, and taking
afternoon naps, that you have forgotten
to ask for the things you really want to know.
What the devil has the time of day got to do with you?
Unless hours were cups of wine, and minutes
chickens, and clocks the tongues of brothel keepers, and dials
the signs of their brothels, and the blessed sun itself
a saucy hot lass in a flame coloured petticoat,
I can't see any reason why you would be so interested
in the time of day.

FAL.
Indeed, you come near me now, Hal; for we that take purses go
by the Moon and the seven stars, and not by Phoebus,--he, that
wandering knight so fair. And I pr'ythee, sweet wag, when thou
art king,--as, God save thy Grace--Majesty I should say, for
grace
thou wilt have none,--

You're getting warm now, Hal, for we who

14

steal purses follow the moon and the seven stars,
and not Phoebus, that fair wandering knight.
And I pray, sweet lad, that when you are king,
as which, God save your grace - Majesty, I should say,
as you won't have any grace-

PRINCE.
What, none?

What, none?

FAL.
No, by my troth; not so much as will serve to be prologue
to an egg and butter.

No, I swear, not enough to say grace for a buttered egg.

PRINCE.
Well, how then? come, roundly, roundly.

What is it then? Get to the point.

FAL.
Marry, then, sweet wag, when thou art king, let not us that
are squires of the night's body be called thieves of the day's
beauty:let us be Diana's foresters, gentlemen of the shade,
minions of the Moon; and let men say we be men of good
government, being governed, as the sea is, by our noble and
chaste mistress the Moon, under whose countenance we steal.

Well then, sweet lad, when you are king, don't let we who are
active by night be accused of being lazy in the day.
Let us be rangers for Diana, attendants of the shadows,
servants of the moon; and let men say we are well ruled men,
being governed by our noble mistress the moon as the sea is,
and we steal under her gaze.

PRINCE.
Thou say'st well, and it holds well too; for the fortune of
us that are the Moon's men doth ebb and flow like the sea,
being governed, as the sea is, by the Moon. As, for proof, now: A
purse of gold most resolutely snatch'd on Monday night, and most
dissolutely spent on Tuesday morning; got with swearing Lay by,
and spent with crying Bring in; now ill as low an ebb as the foot

of the ladder, and by-and-by in as high a flow as the ridge of the
gallows.

You're speaking well, and it's the truth; for the fate of
we who are the moon's men ebbs and flows like the tide,
as we are ruled, like the sea, by the moon. To prove this:
a purse of gold that's well stolen on Monday night, and
profligately spent by Tuesday morning, got by shouting "Stand and deliver"
and spent by shouting, "Bring the drink!" brings one to the low tide of
the foot of the ladder, and soon you'll climb as high as the summit
of the gallows.

FAL.
By the Lord, thou say'st true, lad. And is not my hostess of the
tavern a most sweet wench?

By God, you're telling the truth, lad. And isn't the landlady
the sweetest lass?

PRINCE.
As the honey of Hybla, my old lad of the castle. And is not a
buff jerkin a most sweet robe of durance?

Sweet as the honey of Sicily, my old lad of the castle. and isn't
a convict's uniform the sweetest outfit?

FAL.
How now, how now, mad wag! what, in thy quips and thy
quiddities? what a plague have I to do with a buff jerkin?

What, what, mad lad? What are you saying with your subtle jokes?
What the devil has a convict's uniform to do with me?

PRINCE.
Why, what a pox have I to do with my hostess of the tavern?

Well, what the devil have I to do with the landlady?

FAL.
Well, thou hast call'd her to a reckoning many a time and oft.

Well, you've paid her bill often enough.

PRINCE.
Did I ever call for thee to pay thy part?

Did I ever ask you to pay your share?

FAL.
No; I'll give thee thy due, thou hast paid all there.

No, I'll give you that, you paid the lot there.

PRINCE.
Yea, and elsewhere, so far as my coin would stretch;
and where it would not, I have used my credit.

*Yes, and other places, as much as I could afford;
and when I couldn't, I used my credit.*

FAL.
Yea, and so used it, that, were it not here apparent that
thou art heir-apparent--But I pr'ythee, sweet wag, shall there be
gallows standing in England when thou art king? and
resolution thus fobb'd as it is with the rusty curb of old father
antic the law? Do not thou, when thou art king, hang a thief.

*Yes, so much so, that if it wasn't obvious that
you were the heir-apparent- but I ask you, sweet lad, will there be
gallows standing in England when you are king? And
will brave lads be constrained as they are now by the dull
mad old laws? When you're king, don't hang thieves.*

PRINCE.
No; thou shalt.

No, but you will do some hanging.

FAL.
Shall I? O rare! By the Lord, I'll be a brave judge.

Shall I? Splendid! By God, I'll make a fine judge.

PRINCE.
Thou judgest false already: I mean, thou shalt have the
hanging of the thieves, and so become a rare hangman.

You're already getting it wrong; I mean, you shall make sure
thieves are hung, and so you'll hang well.

FAL.
Well, Hal, well; and in some sort it jumps with my humour;
as well as waiting in the Court, I can tell you.

Good, Hal, good; in some ways that suits me;
it'll be as good as waiting in court, I can tell you.

PRINCE.
For obtaining of suits?

Waiting to get your suit?

FAL.
Yea, for obtaining of suits, whereof the hangman hath no
lean wardrobe. 'Sblood, I am as melancholy as a gib-cat or a
lugg'd bear.

Yes, to get my suit, which the hangman has a good
stock of.By God, I am as depressed as a castrated cat or a
tormented bear.

PRINCE.
Or an old lion, or a lover's lute.

Or an old lion, or a lover's lute.

FAL.
Yea, or the drone of a Lincolnshire bagpipe.

Yes, or a moaning Lincolnshire bagpipe.

PRINCE.
What say'st thou to a hare, or the melancholy of Moor-ditch?

What about a hare, or a filthy sewer by the Thames?

FAL.
Thou hast the most unsavoury similes, and art, indeed, the
most comparative, rascalliest, sweet young prince,--But, Hal, I
pr'ythee trouble me no more with vanity. I would to God thou and
I knew where a commodity of good names were to be bought. An old

lord of the Council rated me the other day in the street about you, sir,--but I mark'd him not; and yet he talk'd very wisely,--but I regarded him not; and yet he talk'd wisely, and in the street too.

Your similes are extremely filthy, and indeed you are
the cheekiest, most rascally, sweet young prince.But, Hal,
please don't bother me with these trifles.I wish to God you and
I knew where one could purchase a good reputation.An old
lord of the Council had a go at me in the street the other day about you,
sir, - I didn't pay him any mind, though he spoke very wisely- but
I didn't pay attention, though he talked wisely, and in the street, too.

PRINCE.
Thou didst well; for wisdom cries out in the streets, and no man regards it.

You did well, for there's plenty of wisdom in the streets, and
nobody pays it any mind.

FAL.
O, thou hast damnable iteration, and art, indeed, able to corrupt a saint.
Thou hast done much harm upon me, Hal; God forgive thee for it! Before I knew thee, Hal, I knew nothing; and now am I, if a man should speak truly, little better than one of the wicked. I must give over this life, and I will give it over; by the Lord, an I do not, I am a villain:I'll be damn'd for never a king's son in Christendom.

Oh, you're a wicked quoter of texts, and you could corrupt a saint.
You've done me a lot of harm, Hal; may God forgive you for it!
Before I knew you, Hal, I knew nothing; and now I am, if we're
honest, almost a bad man.I must
chuck in this life, and I shall; by God, if I don't,
then I'm a villain: I'll not risk damnation for any king's son in Christendom.

PRINCE.
Where shall we take a purse to-morrow, Jack?

Where shall we go stealing tomorrow, Jack?

FAL.
Zounds, where thou wilt, lad; I'll make one:an I do not, call me villain, and baffle me.

By heaven, wherever you like, lad; I'll find somewhere:
if I don't, call me a villain, and disgrace me.

PRINCE.
I see a good amendment of life in thee,--from praying to
purse-taking.

I see you're making a good change of lifestyle - going from praying
to purse-stealing.

FAL.
Why, Hal, 'tis my vocation, Hal; 'tis no sin for a man to labour
in his vocation.

[Enter Pointz.]

--Pointz!--Now shall we know if Gadshill have set a match. O, if
men were to be saved by merit, what hole in Hell were hot enough
for him? This is the most omnipotent villain that ever cried
Stand! to a true man.

Why, Hal, it's my calling, lad; it's not a sin for a man
to work at his calling.

Pointz!Now we shall know if Gadshill has arranged a robbery.Oh, if
men were saved on merit, what pit of hell would be hot enough for him?
He's the most complete villain who ever cried "Stand and deliver"
to an honest man.

PRINCE.
Good morrow, Ned.

Good day, Ned.

POINTZ.
Good morrow, sweet Hal.--What says Monsieur Remorse? what
says Sir John Sack-and-sugar? Jack, how agrees the Devil and
thee about thy soul, that thou soldest him on Good-Friday last
for a cup of Madeira and a cold capon's leg?

Good day, sweet Hal.- What does Mr.Repentance say?What does
Sir John wine-with-sugar say?Jack, what's the arrangement
between you and the devil about your soul, which you sold him

last Good Friday for a cup of Madeira and a cold chicken leg?

PRINCE.
Sir John stands to his word,--the Devil shall have his bargain;
for he was never yet a breaker of proverbs,--he will give the
Devil his due.

Sir John keeps his word - the Devil's price shall be paid;
he never went against a proverb - he will give the
Devil his due.

POINTZ.
Then art thou damn'd for keeping thy word with the Devil.

Then you are damned for keeping your promise to the Devil.

PRINCE.
Else he had been damn'd for cozening the Devil.

Otherwise he would be damned for cheating the devil.

POINTZ.
But, my lads, my lads, to-morrow morning, by four o'clock,
early at Gads-hill! there are pilgrims gong to Canterbury
with rich offerings, and traders riding to London with fat
purses: I have visards for you all; you have horses for
yourselves:Gadshill lies to-night in Rochester:I have bespoke
supper to-morrow night in Eastcheap:we may do it as secure as
sleep. If you will go, I will stuff your purses full of crowns;
if you will not, tarry at home and be hang'd.

But, my lads, my lads, tomorrow morning, at four o'clock,
be early to Gad's Hill!There are pilgrims going to Canterbury
with rich donations, and traders coming to London with fat
purses: I have masks for all of you; you have your own horses;
Gadshill is stopping at Rochester tonight: I have ordered
supper in Eastcheap tomorrow night: we can do it
safe as sleeping.If you come, I will fill your purses with money;
if you won't, stay at home and be hanged.

FAL.
Hear ye, Yedward; if I tarry at home and go not, I'll hang you
for going.

Listen to me, Edward; if I stay at home and don't show, I'll
hang you for going.

POINTZ.
You will, chops?

Will you, fatty?

FAL.
Hal, wilt thou make one?

Hal, will you join us?

PRINCE.
Who, I rob? I a thief? not I, by my faith.

What, me steal? Be a thief? I swear I won't.

FAL.
There's neither honesty, manhood, nor good fellowship in thee,
nor thou camest not of the blood royal, if thou darest not stand
for ten shillings.

There's no honesty, manhood or friendliness in you,
and you can't have royal blood, if you're afraid to hold
somebody up for ten shillings.

PRINCE.
Well, then, once in my days I'll be a madcap.

Well then, for once in my life I'll be reckless.

FAL.
Why, that's well said.

Good for you.

PRINCE.
Well, come what will, I'll tarry at home.

But whatever happens, I'm stopping at home.

FAL.
By the Lord, I'll be a traitor, then, when thou art king.

Then I swear when you're king I'll be a traitor.

PRINCE.
I care not.

I don't care.

POINTZ.

Sir John, I pr'ythee, leave the Prince and me alone: I will
lay him down such reasons for this adventure, that he shall go.

*Sir John, I beg you, leave me and the prince alone: I will
show him such good reasons for this adventure that he will come.*

FAL.
Well, God give thee the spirit of persuasion, and him the ears
of profiting, that what thou speakest may move, and what he
hears may be believed, that the true Prince may, for recreation-
sake, prove a false thief; for the poor abuses of the time want
countenance. Farewell; you shall find me in Eastcheap.

*Good, may God give you the skills to persuade, and him the ears
to listen to what's good for him, so that what you say moves him,
and so he believes what he hears, so that the true Prince may, for fun,
be a dishonest thief; for the injustices of the time want
sorting out.Farewell; you'll find me in Eastcheap.*

PRINCE.
Farewell, thou latter Spring! farewell, All-hallown Summer!

Farewell, you late spring.Farewell, you Indian summer!

[Exit Falstaff.]

POINTZ.
Now, my good sweet honey-lord, ride with us to-morrow:I
have a jest to execute that I cannot manage alone. Falstaff,
Bardolph, Peto, and Gadshill, shall rob those men that we have
already waylaid:yourself and I will not be there; and when they
have the booty, if you and I do not rob them, cut this head off
from my shoulders.

Now, my good sweet as honey lord, ride with us tomorrow: I
have a joke to play that I can't do alone.Falstaff,
Bardolph, Peto and Gadshill will rob these men we have already
planned for: you and I will not be there; and when they have the plunder,
if you and I can't then rob them, chop my head off.

PRINCE.
But how shall we part with them in setting forth?

But how will we split away from them?

POINTZ.
Why, we will set forth before or after them, and appoint them
a place of meeting, wherein it is at our pleasure to fail; and
then will they adventure upon the exploit themselves; which they
shall have no sooner achieved but we'll set upon them.

Why, we'll set out before or after them, and arrange to meet
them somewhere, and we won't turn up; and
then they will take on the job themselves; and no sooner
than they've done it we'll attack them.

PRINCE.
Ay, but 'tis like that they will know us by our horses, by our
habits, and by every other appointment, to be ourselves.

Yes, but they'll probably recognise us by our horses, our
clothes, and every other sign.

POINTZ.
Tut! our horses they shall not see,--I'll tie them in the wood;
our visards we will change, after we leave them; and, sirrah, I
have cases of buckram for the nonce, to immask our noted
outward garments.

Tut!They won't see our horses - I'll tie them up in the wood;
we'll change our masks, after we have seen them; and, sir, I
have canvas overalls which we can use to cover up
our identifiable clothes.

PRINCE.
But I doubt they will be too hard for us.

But surely we can't overpower them?

POINTZ.

Well, for two of them, I know them to be as true-bred cowards as ever turn'd back; and for the third, if he fight longer than he sees reason, I'll forswear arms. The virtue of this jest will be, the incomprehensible lies that this same fat rogue will tell us when we meet at supper: how thirty, at least, he fought with; what wards, what blows, what extremities he endured; and in the reproof of this lies the jest.

Well, I know that two of them are the biggest cowards who ever ran away; as for the third, if he fights when he sees he can't win, I'll give up fighting. The great thing in this joke will be listening to the incredible lies of this fat rogue when we meet at supper; how he fought at least thirty men; what defence, what attacks, what terrible things he suffered; showing him to be a liar will be the joke.

PRINCE.

Well, I'll go with thee:provide us all things necessary and meet me to-night in Eastcheap; there I'll sup. Farewell.

Well, I'll go with you: get all the things we need and meet me tonight in Eastcheap; I'll dine there.Farewell.

POINTZ.

Farewell, my lord.

Farewell, my lord.

[Exit.]

PRINCE.

I know you all, and will awhile uphold
The unyok'd humour of your idleness:
Yet herein will I imitate the Sun,
Who doth permit the base contagious clouds
To smother-up his beauty from the world,
That, when he please again to be himself,
Being wanted, he may be more wonder'd at,
By breaking through the foul and ugly mists
Of vapours that did seem to strangle him.
If all the year were playing holidays,
To sport would be as tedious as to work;

But, when they seldom come, they wish'd-for come,
And nothing pleaseth but rare accidents.
So, when this loose behaviour I throw off,
And pay the debt I never promised,
By how much better than my word I am,
By so much shall I falsify men's hopes;
And, like bright metal on a sullen ground,
My reformation, glittering o'er my fault,
Shall show more goodly and attract more eyes
Than that which hath no foil to set it off.
I'll so offend, to make offence a skill;
Redeeming time, when men think least I will.

I know what you're all like, and for a while
I'll tolerate your lazy unchecked desires:
but in doing this I'll be like the sun,
who allows low pestilent clouds
to hide his beauty from the world,
so that when he wants to be himself again
he is more loved through his absence,
when he breaks through the foul ugly mist
and fog which seemed to strangle him.
If every day of the year was a holiday,
play would be as dull as work;
but when you don't have many, you look forward to them,
and nothing pleases like something out of the ordinary.
So, when I put a stop to this immoral behaviour,
and fulfil the promise I don't show now,
I shall be much better than men think,
I'll lower all their expectations;
like bright metal on a dull background,
my reformation, shining against my faults,
will look better and attract more people
than something which has no contrast to set it off.
I'll offend in a way which will be beneficial,
making amends when men least expect it.

[Exit.]

Scene III. The Same. A Room in the Palace.

[Enter King Henry, Northumberland, Worcester, Hotspur, Sir Walter Blunt, and others.]

KING.
My blood hath been too cold and temperate,
Unapt to stir at these indignities,
And you have found me; for, accordingly,
You tread upon my patience:but be sure
I will from henceforth rather be myself,
Mighty and to be fear'd, than my condition,
Which hath been smooth as oil, soft as young down,
And therefore lost that title of respect
Which the proud soul ne'er pays but to the proud.

I have been too patient and calm,
not reacting to these outrages,
and you have found me so; for you
are abusing my patience: but rest assured
from now on I will fit my position,
be mighty and fearsome, rather than follow my nature,
which has made me smooth as oil, soft as ducklings' feathers,
and so I have lost the respect
which the proud only ever give to their own kind.

WOR.
Our House, my sovereign liege, little deserves
The scourge of greatness to be used on it;
And that same greatness too which our own hands
Have holp to make so portly.

Our family, my royal lord, hardly deserves
to be attacked with such greatness;
the same greatness which we ourselves
helped to its current position.

NORTH.
My good lord,--

27

My good lord-

KING.
Worcester, get thee gone; for I do see
Danger and disobedience in thine eye:
O, sir, your presence is too bold and peremptory,
And majesty might never yet endure
The moody frontier of a servant brow.
You have good leave to leave us:when we need
Your use and counsel, we shall send for you.

[Exit Worcester.]

[To Northumberland.]

You were about to speak.

Worcester, get out; for I can see
threats and disobedience in your eyes:
oh, sir, you are too arrogant and bossy,
and a king might never see again such
angry defiance in a subject's frown.
You have my permission to go: when I need
you or your advice, I'll send for you.

You were about to speak.

NORTH.
Yea, my good lord.
Those prisoners in your Highness' name demanded,
Which Harry Percy here at Holmedon took,
Were, as he says, not with such strength denied
As is deliver'd to your Majesty:
Either envy, therefore, or misprision
Is guilty of this fault, and not my son.

Yes, my good lord.
Those prisoners which your Majesty requested,
which Harry Percy captured here at Holmedon;
he didn't, he says, deny your request in such
strong terms as your majesty has been told:
it's either jealousy or some misunderstanding that has
created this fault, not my son.

HOT.

My liege, I did deny no prisoners.
But, I remember, when the fight was done,
When I was dry with rage and extreme toil,
Breathless and faint, leaning upon my sword,
Came there a certain lord, neat, trimly dress'd,
Fresh as a bridegroom; and his chin new reap'd
Show'd like a stubble-land at harvest-home:
He was perfumed like a milliner;
And 'twixt his finger and his thumb he held
A pouncet-box, which ever and anon
He gave his nose, and took't away again;
Who therewith angry, when it next came there,
Took it in snuff:and still he smiled and talk'd;
And, as the soldiers bore dead bodies by,
He call'd them untaught knaves, unmannerly,
To bring a slovenly unhandsome corse
Betwixt the wind and his nobility.
With many holiday and lady terms
He question'd me; amongst the rest, demanded
My prisoners in your Majesty's behalf.
I then, all smarting with my wounds being cold,
Out of my grief and my impatience
To be so pester'd with a popinjay,
Answer'd neglectingly, I know not what,--
He should, or he should not; for't made me mad
To see him shine so brisk, and smell so sweet,
And talk so like a waiting-gentlewoman
Of guns and drums and wounds,--God save the mark!--
And telling me the sovereign'st thing on Earth
Was parmaceti for an inward bruise;
And that it was great pity, so it was,
This villainous salt-petre should be digg'd
Out of the bowels of the harmless earth,
Which many a good tall fellow had destroy'd
So cowardly; and, but for these vile guns,
He would himself have been a soldier.
This bald unjointed chat of his, my lord,
I answered indirectly, as I said;
And I beseech you, let not his report
Come current for an accusation
Betwixt my love and your high Majesty.

My Lord, I didn't refuse to deliver any prisoners,

but I remember, when the battle was over,
when I was dry with rage, and extreme effort,
breathless and faint, leaning upon my sword,
a certain Lord came, neatly and primly dressed,
fresh as a bridegroom, with his newly shaved chin
looking like a cornfield at harvest time.
He was perfumed like a haberdasher,
and between his finger and thumb he held
a scent box, which every now and again
he held to his nose, and then removed–
and then the next time his nose was offended
he took it as snuff–and still he smiled and talked:
and as the soldiers carried the dead bodies past,
he called them ignorant knaves, ill mannered,
for bringing dirty ugly corpses into the presence of his nobility.
He questioned me with many highflown
terms, and in the process demanded
my prisoners on your Majesty's behalf.
Then I, suffering from my wounds,
being pestered with such a prattler,
answered without thinking, I don't know what,
he should or shouldn't do, for it made me angry
to see him shining so brightly and smelling so sweet,
talking like a lady's maid
about guns, and drums, and wounds, God help us!
He told me that the best thing on earth
for internal bruising was spermaceti,
and that it was a great pity, indeed it was,
that evil saltpetre should be dug
out of the innards of the harmless earth,
destroying so many good tall fellows
in such a cowardly way, and that if it wasn't for these horrible guns
he would have been a soldier himself.
This empty rambling chat of his, my lord,
I answered without thinking, as I said,
and I beg you, don't let his report
be used to accuse me of lacking
in any love for your high Majesty.

BLUNT.
The circumstance consider'd, good my lord,
Whatever Harry Percy then had said
To such a person, and in such a place,

At such a time, with all the rest re-told,
May reasonably die, and never rise
To do him wrong, or any way impeach
What then he said, so he unsay it now.

When you consider the circumstances, my good lord,
whatever Harry Percy had said then
to such a person, and in such a place,
at such a time, with everything else that's been said,
can reasonably be forgotten, and never used
against him, or to charge him in any way
for what he said, as he retracts it now.

KING.
Why, yet he doth deny his prisoners,
But with proviso and exception,
That we at our own charge shall ransom straight
His brother-in-law, the foolish Mortimer;
Who, on my soul, hath wilfully betray'd
The lives of those that he did lead to fight
Against that great magician, damn'd Glendower,
Whose daughter, as we hear, the Earl of March
Hath lately married. Shall our coffers, then,
Be emptied to redeem a traitor home?
Shall we buy treason? and indent with fears
When they have lost and forfeited themselves?
No, on the barren mountains let him starve;
For I shall never hold that man my friend
Whose tongue shall ask me for one penny cost
To ransom home revolted Mortimer.

Yes, but he still withholds the prisoners,
laying down the condition that
I should at my own expense ransom at once
his brother-in-law, the foolish Mortimer;
someone who, I swear, willfully betrayed
the lives of the oneshe led in battle
against that great magician, damned Glendower,
whose daughter, we're told, the Earl of March
has recently married. So should I empty my
treasure chests to bring home a traitor?
Should I pay for treason? And make an agreement
for those who have lost and forfeited themselves?
No, let him starve on the barren mountains;

I won't think of any man as my friend
if he asks me to pay one penny
in ransom for the rebel Mortimer.

HOT.
Revolted Mortimer!
He never did fall off, my sovereign liege,
But by the chance of war:to prove that true
Needs no more but one tongue for all those wounds,
Those mouthed wounds, which valiantly he took,
When on the gentle Severn's sedgy bank,
In single opposition, hand to hand,
He did confound the best part of an hour
In changing hardiment with great Glendower.
Three times they breathed, and three times did they drink,
Upon agreement, of swift Severn's flood;
Who then, affrighted with their bloody looks,
Ran fearfully among the trembling reeds,
And hid his crisp head in the hollow bank
Blood-stained with these valiant combatants.
Never did base and rotten policy
Colour her working with such deadly wounds;
Nor never could the noble Mortimer
Receive so many, and all willingly:
Then let not him be slander'd with revolt.

The rebel Mortimer!
He never let you down, my royal lord,
except through thechances of war: that can be proved
just by hearing about all those wounds,
those gaping wounds, which he bravely took,
when on the grassy banks of the sweet Severn
he rebuffed great Glendower
for the best part of an hour, matching
his bravery in single combat.
They paused for breath three times, and to drink
by agreement from the waters of the Severn,
which was so frightened by their bloody appearance,
that it ran fearfully amongst its trembling reeds,
and hid its rippling head under the hollow banks,
stained with the blood of these brave fighters.
No wretched or rotten cunning
ever risked receiving such deadly wounds,
and the noble Mortimer could not

have taken so many, and all of them willingly:
so don't let him be accused of rebellion.

King.
Thou dost belie him, Percy, thou dost belie him;
He never did encounter with Glendower:
I tell thee,
He durst as well have met the Devil alone
As Owen Glendower for an enemy.
Art not ashamed? But, sirrah, henceforth
Let me not hear you speak of Mortimer:
Send me your prisoners with the speediest means,
Or you shall hear in such a kind from me
As will displease you.--My Lord Northumberland,
We license your departure with your son.--
Send us your prisoners, or you'll hear of it.

You are lying for him, Percy, lying,
he never fought Glendower:
I tell you, he might as well have met the devil in single combat
as to fight with Owen Glendower.
Are you not ashamed? But Sir, from now on
don't let me hear you speak of Mortimer:
send me your prisoners by the quickest way possible,
or you shall hear from me in such a way
that you won't like it. My Lord Northumberland:
I give you permission to leave with your son.
Send us your prisoners, or you will hear of it.

[Exeunt King Henry, Blunt, and train.]

HOT.
An if the Devil come and roar for them,
I will not send them:I will after straight,
And tell him so; for I will ease my heart,
Although it be with hazard of my head.

And if the devil came and asked for them,
I wouldn't send them: I'll follow after him,
and tell him so; for I will ease my heart,
even though it's at the risk of my head.

NORTH.
What, drunk with choler? stay, and pause awhile:

Here comes your uncle.

What, are you drunk with anger? Wait, pause awhile:
here comes your uncle.

[Re-enter Worcester.]

HOT.
Speak of Mortimer!
Zounds, I will speak of him; and let my soul
Want mercy, if I do not join with him:
Yea, on his part I'll empty all these veins,
And shed my dear blood drop by drop i' the dust,
But I will lift the down-trod Mortimer
As high i' the air as this unthankful King,
As this ingrate and canker'd Bolingbroke.

Speak of Mortimer!
By God, I will speak of him; and may my soul
not find mercy, if I do not help him:
for him I will empty all these veins,
and let my dear blood run drop by drop into the dust,
but I will lift the downtrodden Mortimer
as high in the air as this thankless King
as this ungrateful and rotten Bolingbroke.

NORTH.
[To Worcester.]
Brother, the King hath made your nephew mad.

Brother, the King has made your nephew mad.

WOR.
Who struck this heat up after I was gone?

Who stirred up this anger after I was gone?

HOT.
He will, forsooth, have all my prisoners;
And when I urged the ransom once again
Of my wife's brother, then his cheek look'd pale,
And on my face he turn'd an eye of death,
Trembling even at the name of Mortimer.

By God, he wants all my prisoners;
and when I once again asked him to ransom
my wife's brother, then he went pale,
and he turned a deathly look on me,
trembling even at the name of Mortimer.

WOR.

I cannot blame him:was not he proclaim'd
By Richard that dead is the next of blood?

I can't blame him: wasn't he announced
by dead Richard as the next in line?

NORTH.

He was; I heard the proclamation:
And then it was when the unhappy King--
Whose wrongs in us God pardon!--did set forth
Upon his Irish expedition;
From whence he intercepted did return
To be deposed, and shortly murdered.

He was; I heard the announcement:
and it was then that the unhappy king–
May God forgive us for his sins!–Set out
on his Irish expedition;
from which he was intercepted and returned
to be overthrown, and quickly murdered.

WOR.

And for whose death we in the world's wide mouth
Live scandalized and foully spoken of.

And for the death of whom we are widely
condemned and foully spoken of.

HOT.

But, soft! I pray you; did King Richard then
Proclaim my brother Edmund Mortimer
Heir to the crown?

But, wait! Tell me please; did King Richard
proclaim that my brother Edmund Mortimer
was the heir to the crown?

NORTH.

He did; myself did hear it.

He did; I heard it myself.

HOT.

Nay, then I cannot blame his cousin King,
That wish'd him on the barren mountains starve.
But shall it be, that you, that set the crown
Upon the head of this forgetful man,
And for his sake wear the detested blot
Of murderous subornation,--shall it be,
That you a world of curses undergo,
Being the agents, or base second means,
The cords, the ladder, or the hangman rather?--
O, pardon me, that I descend so low,
To show the line and the predicament
Wherein you range under this subtle King;--
Shall it, for shame, be spoken in these days,
Or fill up chronicles in time to come,
That men of your nobility and power
Did gage them both in an unjust behalf,--
As both of you, God pardon it! have done,--
To put down Richard, that sweet lovely rose,
And plant this thorn, this canker, Bolingbroke?
And shall it, in more shame, be further spoken,
That you are fool'd, discarded, and shook off
By him for whom these shames ye underwent?
No! yet time serves, wherein you may redeem
Your banish'd honours, and restore yourselves
Into the good thoughts of the world again;
Revenge the jeering and disdain'd contempt
Of this proud King, who studies day and night
To answer all the debt he owes to you
Even with the bloody payment of your deaths:
Therefore, I say,--

No, then I cannot blame his cousin the King,
for wanting him to starve on the barren mountains.
But it may be that you who put the crown
on the head of this forgetful man,
and who for his sake wear the revolting stain
of murderous disobedience–is it the case
that you suffer a world of curses,

36

being the agents, or the low seconders,
the rope, the ladder, or are you the hangman?
Oh, pardon me, that I speak so basely
to show you the position and danger
you are in under the rule of this cunning King!
Will it be spoken of with shame now,
or in the histories of times to come,
that men of your own ability and power
both fought for an unjust cause
(as both of you, God forgive you, have done)
to throw down Richard, that sweet lovely rose,
and plant this thorn bush, this rotten Bolingbroke?
And shall it be further said, more shamefully,
that you were tricked, ignored, rejected
by the one for whom you undertook such a shame?
No, there is still time for you to recover
your lost honour, and put yourselves
back into the good thoughts of the world:
revenge the jeering and disdainful contempt
of this proud king, who is thinking day and night
of how to repay the debt he owes you,
which he shall repay with your bloody deaths:
therefore, I say–

WOR.
Peace, cousin, say no more:
And now I will unclasp a secret book,
And to your quick-conceiving discontent
I'll read you matter deep and dangerous;
As full of peril and adventurous spirit
As to o'er-walk a current roaring loud
On the unsteadfast footing of a spear.

Peace, cousin, say no more:
I will now reveal a secret matter,
and to your hasty discontent
I'll tell you about deep and dangerous things;
as full of danger and adventure
as trying to walk over roaring torrent
just balancing on an unsteady spear.

HOT.
If we fall in, good night, or sink or swim!
Send danger from the east unto the west,

So honour cross it from the north to south,
And let them grapple. O, the blood more stirs
To rouse a lion than to start a hare!

If we fall in, good night, sink or swim!
Send danger from the East to the West,
so that honour can cross it from the North to South,
and let them fight: it's more exciting
to hunt a lion than a hare.

NORTH.
Imagination of some great exploit
Drives him beyond the bounds of patience.

Imagining some great exploit
is making him hotheaded.

HOT.
By Heaven, methinks it were an easy leap,
To pluck bright honour from the pale-faced Moon;
Or dive into the bottom of the deep,
Where fathom-line could never touch the ground,
And pluck up drowned honour by the locks;
So he that doth redeem her thence might wear
Without corrival all her dignities:
But out upon this half-faced fellowship!

By heaven, I think it would be an easy task
to go and steal the light of honour from the pale faced moon;
or to dive to the bottom of the ocean,
were thedepths could never be measured,
and pull up ground on by its hair;
so that the one who saved her could then
lay claim to the badge of honour:
but I'm dammed if I'll share it!

WOR.
He apprehends a world of figures here,
But not the form of what he should attend.--
Good cousin, give me audience for a while.

It's all very well him talking,
but he doesn't understand the substance–
good cousin, listen to me for a while.

HOT.
I cry you mercy.

Please excuse me.

WOR.
Those same noble Scots
That are your prisoners,--

Those noble Scots
who are your prisoners–

HOT.
I'll keep them all;
By God, he shall not have a Scot of them;
No, if a Scot would save his soul, he shall not:
I'll keep them, by this hand.

I'll keep them all;
by God, he shall not have one of them,
not if he needed one to save his soul, he will not:
I swear that I will keep them.

WOR.
You start away,
And lend no ear unto my purposes.
Those prisoners you shall keep;--

You're rushing off,
and not listening to my point.
You will keep those prisoners–

HOT.
Nay, I will; that's flat.
He said he would not ransom Mortimer;
Forbade my tongue to speak of Mortimer;
But I will find him when he lies asleep,
And in his ear I'll holla Mortimer!
Nay,I'll have a starling shall be taught to speak
Nothing but Mortimer, and give it him,
To keep his anger still in motion.

No, I will, that's flat.

He said he would not ransom Mortimer;
he forbade me from talking of Mortimer;
but I will find him when he's lying asleep,
and in his ear I'll shout "Mortimer!"
No, I'll get a starling and train him to say
nothing but Mortimer, and give it to him,
to make him permanently angry.

WOR.
Hear you, cousin; a word.

Listen, cousin; word.

HOT.
All studies here I solemnly defy,
Save how to gall and pinch this Bolingbroke:
And that same sword-and-buckler Prince of Wales,
But that I think his father loves him not,
And would be glad he met with some mischance,
I'd have him poison'd with a pot of ale.

I solemnly swear I will study nothing else
except how I can annoy and pinch this Bolingbroke:
and that identical swaggerer the Prince of Wales,
except for the fact I think his father doesn't love him,
and would be glad if he met with some accident,
I'd have someone give him some poisoned beer.

WOR.
Farewell, kinsman:I will talk to you
When you are better temper'd to attend.

Farewell, kinsman: I will talk to you
when you are in a more listening mood.

NORTH.
Why, what a wasp-stung and impatient fool
Art thou, to break into this woman's mood,
Tying thine ear to no tongue but thine own!

Why, what a hotheaded and impatient fool
you are, to screech like a woman,
listening to nobody but yourself!

40

HOT.

Why, look you, I am whipp'd and scourged with rods,
Nettled, and stung with pismires, when I hear
Of this vile politician, Bolingbroke.
In Richard's time,--what do you call the place?--
A plague upon't!--it is in Gioucestershire;--
'Twas where the madcap Duke his uncle kept,
His uncle York;--where I first bow'd my knee
Unto this king of smiles, this Bolingbroke;--
When you and he came back from Ravenspurg.

Well, look, I am beaten and cut with rods,
stung with nettles and ants, when I hear
about this vile politician Bolingbroke.
In Richard's time–what do you call the place?
Damn it, it's in Gloucestershire–
where the crazy duke kept his uncle,
his uncle York–that was where I first knelt
to this smiling King, this Bolingbroke,
by God, when you and he came back from Ravenspurgh.

NORTH.

At Berkeley-castle.

At Berkeley Castle.

HOT.

You say true:--
Why, what a candy deal of courtesy
This fawning greyhound then did proffer me!
Look, when his infant fortune came to age,
And, Gentle Harry Percy, and kind cousin,--
O, the Devil take such cozeners!--God forgive me!--
Good uncle, tell your tale; for I have done.

That's right:
well, what a sugary quantity of courtesy
this grovelling dog offered me then!
"See, when his infant fortune comes of age",
and, "gentle Harry Percy", and "kind cousin"–
O, the devil take such deceivers! God forgive me!
Good uncle, tell your tale; I'm finished.

WOR.

Nay, if you have not, to't again;
We'll stay your leisure.

Well, if you haven't, carry on;
we'll wait for you.

HOT.
I have done, i'faith.

I swear, I'm finished.

WOR.
Then once more to your Scottish prisoners.
Deliver them up without their ransom straight,
And make the Douglas' son your only mean
For powers in Scotland; which, for divers reasons
Which I shall send you written, be assured,
Will easily be granted.--
[To Northumberland.] You, my lord,
Your son in Scotland being thus employ'd,
Shall secretly into the bosom creep
Of that same noble prelate, well beloved,
Th' Archbishop.

Then go back to your Scottish prisoners.
Hand them over at once without their ransom,
and make the son of Douglas your only
agent of power in Scotland; for various reasons,
which I shall write to you about, I can assure you,
that will definitely be granted–
[to Northumberland] you, my lord,
while your son is doing this in Scotland
you shall secretly creep into the heart
of that noble clergyman, the well loved
Archbishop.

HOT.
Of York, is't not?

Of York, you mean?

WOR.
True; who bears hard
His brother's death at Bristol, the Lord Scroop.

I speak not this in estimation,
As what I think might be, but what I know
Is ruminated, plotted, and set down,
And only stays but to behold the face
Of that occasion that shall bring it on.

Yes; he has taken his brother's
death at Bristol, the Lord Scroop, very hard.
I'm not just guessing this,
saying I think it might be the case, I know
it has been thought of, plotted and written down,
and is only waiting for the right time
to bring it on.

HOT.
I smell't:upon my life, it will do well.

I can smell it: I swear on my life, it will do well.

NORTH.
Before the game's a-foot, thou still lett'st slip.

But you are unleashing the hounds before the game is running.

HOT.
Why, it cannot choose but be a noble plot:--
And then the power of Scotland and of York
To join with Mortimer, ha?

Well, it can't help be a noble plot:
and then the power of Scotland and of York
will join with Mortimer, yes?

WOR.
And so they shall.

Yes they shall.

HOT.
In faith, it is exceedingly well aim'd.

By God, this is very well-planned.

WOR.

And 'tis no little reason bids us speed,
To save our heads by raising of a head;
For, bear ourselves as even as we can,
The King will always think him in our debt,
And think we think ourselves unsatisfied,
Till he hath found a time to pay us home:
And see already how he doth begin
To make us strangers to his looks of love.

And we've got very good reason to be hasty,
to save our heads by raising an army;
for, however reasonable we are,
the King would always think of himself as being in our debt,
and think that we are not satisfied,
until he has found a way to finish us off:
you can already see how he's beginning
to ostracise us from his love.

HOT.
He does, he does:we'll be revenged on him.

He is, he is, we'll have revenge on him.

WOR.
Cousin, farewell:no further go in this
Than I by letters shall direct your course.
When time is ripe,-- which will be suddenly,--
I'll steal to Glendower and Lord Mortimer;
Where you and Douglas, and our powers at once,
As I will fashion it, shall happily meet,
To bear our fortunes in our own strong arms,
Which now we hold at much uncertainty.

Cousin, farewell. Don't do anything more
than what I instruct you by letter.
When the time comes, and it will be sudden,
I'll go secretly to Glendower, and Lord Mortimer,
where you, and Douglas, and all of our forces together,
as I plan it, will happily meet,
to take our fortunes into our own strong hands,
to end the uncertainty we have now.

NORTH.
Farewell, good brother:we shall thrive, I trust.

Farewell, good brother: I hope we shall succeed.

HOT.
Uncle, adieu: O, let the hours be short,
Till fields and blows and groans applaud our sport!

Uncle, goodbye: oh, don't let it be long
until battlefields and blows and groans applaud our efforts!

[Exeunt.]

Act II

Scene I. Rochester. An Inn-Yard.

[Enter a Carrier with a lantern in his hand.]

1. CAR.
Heigh-ho! an't be not four by the day, I'll be hang'd:
Charles' wain is over the new chimney, and yet our horse' not
pack'd.--What, ostler!

*Come on! If it's not already four in the morning I'll be
hanged; the Great Bear is over the new chimney, and
our horse is still not loaded. Hello, stableman!*

OST.
[within.] Anon, anon.

In a minute.

1. CAR.
I pr'ythee, Tom, beat Cut's saddle, put a few flocks in the
point; the poor jade is wrung in the withers out of all cess.

*And please Tom, plump up the horse's saddle and put some wool
in the pommel; the poor nag has calluses all over its shoulders.*

[Enter another Carrier.]

2. CAR.
Peas and beans are as dank here as a dog, and that is the
next way to give poor jades the bots; this house is turned
upside down since Robin ostler died.

*The peas and beans here are as damp as a dog, and that's the
best way to give poor nags worms; this house has been
turned upside down since Robin the ostler died.*

1. CAR.
Poor fellow! never joyed since the price of oats rose; it was
the death of him.

Poor fellow! He had never been happy since the price of oats went up; it was the death of him.

2. CAR.
I think this be the most villainous house in all London road
for fleas:I am stung like a tench.

*I think this must be the worst house on the London Road
for fleas, I'm stung like a tench.*

1. CAR.
Like a tench! by the Mass, there is ne'er a king in Christendom
could be better bit than I have been since the first cock.--What,
ostler! come away and be hang'd; come away.

*Like a tench! By heaven, there isn't a king in Christendom
who could have been bitten better than I have been since midnight–
hello, ostler! Hurry up, and be hanged, hurry up!*

2. CAR.
I have a gammon of bacon and two razes of ginger, to be
delivered as far as Charing-cross.

*I have a joint of bacon and two ginger roots, to be
delivered to Charing Cross.*

1. CAR.
'Odsbody! the turkeys in my pannier are quite starved.--What,
ostler! A plague on thee! hast thou never an eye in thy head?
canst not hear? An 'twere not as good a deed as drink to break
the pate of thee, I am a very villain. Come, and be hang'd:
hast no faith in thee?

*My God! The turkeys in my basket are quite starved.–What,
ostler! A plague on you! Don't you have eyes in your head?
Can't you hear? If it's not as good a thing to break your head as it is
to have a drink, I'm a villain. Hurry up, and be hanged:
can't you do anything?*

[Enter Gadshill.]

GADS.
Good morrow, carriers. What's o'clock?

Good day, carriers. What's the time?

1. CAR.
I think it be two o'clock.

I think it's two o'clock.

GADS.
I pr'ythee, lend me thy lantern, to see my gelding in the stable.

Please, lend me your lantern, so I can see my gelding in the stable.

1. CAR.
Nay, soft, I pray ye; I know a trick worth two of that, i'faith.

No, please be quiet; I'm not such a fool as that.

GADS.
I pr'ythee, lend me thine.

I'm asking, lend me yours.

2. CAR.
Ay, when? canst tell? Lend me thy lantern, quoth a? marry, I'll see thee hang'd first.

What's that? Eh? Lend me your lantern, he says? I swear, I'll see you hanged first.

GADS.
Sirrah carrier, what time do you mean to come to London?

Mr Carrier, what time do you intend to arrive in London?

2. CAR.
Time enough to go to bed with a candle, I warrant thee.--
Come, neighbour Muggs, we'll call up the gentlemen:they will along with company, for they have great charge.

In time to go to bed with a candle, I promise you.
Come, neighbour Muggs, we'll call the gentlemen; they will want to come along with us, for they have a valuable cargo.

[Exeunt Carriers.]

GADS.
What, ho! chamberlain!

Hello there! Chamberlain!

CHAM.
[Within.] At hand, quoth pick-purse.

I'm ready Sir, as the pickpocket says.

GADS.
That's even as fair as--at hand, quoth the chamberlain; for
thou variest no more from picking of purses than giving
direction doth from labouring; thou lay'st the plot how.

*That's as good as "I'm ready, as the Chamberlain says"; for
you're no more different to a pickpocket than a foreman
is to his labourers; you're the one who plans everything.*

[Enter Chamberlain.]

CHAM.
Good morrow, Master Gadshill. It holds current that I told
you yesternight:there's a franklin in the wild of Kent hath
brought three hundred marks with him in gold:I heard him
tell it to one of his company last night at supper; a kind of
auditor; one that hath abundance of charge too, God knows what.
They are up already, and call for eggs and butter; they will away
presently.

*Good day, Master Gadshill. What I told you yesterday
evening is still true: there's a freeholder in the Weald of Kent who has
brought three hundred marks in gold with him: I heard him
mention it to one of his company last night at supper; he's a kind of
accountant; and one who has plenty of responsibility too, God knows what.
They are already up, and calling for buttered eggs; they will leave
shortly.*

GADS.
Sirrah, if they meet not with Saint Nicholas' clerks, I'll give
thee this neck.

50

Sir, if they don't meet some highwaymen, you can
hang me.

CHAM.
No, I'll none of it: I pr'ythee, keep that for the hangman; for
I know thou worshippest Saint Nicholas as truly as a man of
falsehood may.

No, I'll have none of that: please, keep your neck for the hangman; for
I know that you worship the patron saint of highwaymen as truly as
such a false man can.

GADS.
What talkest thou to me of the hangman? if I hang, I'll make
a fat pair of gallows; for, if I hang, old Sir John hangs with
me, and thou know'st he is no starveling. Tut! there are other
Trojans that thou dreamest not of, the which, for sport-sake,
are content to do the profession some grace; that would, if
matters should be look'd into, for their own credit-sake, make
all whole. I am joined with no foot land-rakers, no long-staff
sixpenny strikers, none of these mad mustachio purple-hued
malt-worms; but with nobility and tranquillity, burgomasters and
great oneyers; such as can hold in, such as will strike sooner
than speak, and speak sooner than drink, and drink sooner than
pray:and yet, zwounds, I lie; for they pray continually to their
saint, the Commonwealth; or, rather, not pray to her, but prey on
her, for they ride up and down on her, and make her their boots.

Why you talking to me about the hangman? If I hang, it'll be
on a fat pair of gallows; because, if I hang, old Sir John will hang with
me, and you know he's no lightweight. Tut! There are other
companions who you don't know about, who, just for fun,
are prepared to do the job properly; they would, if
asked to look into the matter, for the sake of their own credit, do
the whole thing. I don't associate with footpads, thugs
who rob for sixpence, none of these purple faced moustached
boozers; but with noblemen, calm men, mayors and
important officials; ones who can control themselves, who will
strike sooner than speak, and speak sooner than drink, and drink sooner than
pray: and yet, by God, I lie; for they pray continually to their
saint, the Commonwealth; or rather, they don't pray to her, they prey on her,
for they ride up and down on her, making her their booty.

CHAM.
What, the Commonwealth their boots? will she hold out water
in foul way?

What, the Commonwealth is their boots? Will she keep out the water
on muddy roads?

GADS.
She will, she will; justice hath liquor'd her. We steal as in a
castle, cock-sure; we have the receipt of fernseed,--we walk
invisible.

She will, she will; she's been well greased. We steal with
complete impunity; it's as if we've taken the fernseed to make us invisible.

CHAM.
Nay, by my faith, I think you are more beholding to the night
than to fern-seed for your walking invisible.

No, I swear, I think it's the night rather than
fernseed that makes you invisible.

GADS.
Give me thy hand:thou shalt have a share in our purchase, as
I am a true man.

Give me your hand: you shall get us to share of our profits,
as I am an honest man.

CHAM.
Nay, rather let me have it, as you are a false thief.

No, I'd sooner have your promise as a false thief.

GADS.
Go to; homo is a common name to all men. Bid the ostler
bring my gelding out of the stable. Farewell, you muddy knave.

Get away, all men are the same at bottom. Tell the ostler
to bring my gelding out of the stable. Farewell, you muddy knave.

[Exeunt.]

Scene II. The Road by Gads-hill.

[Enter Prince Henry and Pointz; Bardolph and Peto at some distance.]

POINTZ.
Come, shelter, shelter:I have remov'd Falstaff's horse, and he frets like a gumm'd velvet.

Come, hide, hide: I have taken Falstaff's horse away, and he chafes like fraying velvet.

PRINCE.
Stand close.

Keep near me.

[They retire.]

[Enter Falstaff.]

FAL.
Pointz! Pointz, and be hang'd! Pointz!

Pointz!Pointz, damn you!Pointz!

PRINCE.
[Coming forward.]
Peace, ye fat-kidney'd rascal! what a brawling dost thou keep!

Quiet, you tubby rascal!What a racket you're making.

FAL.
Where's Pointz, Hal?

Where's Pointz, Hal?

PRINCE.
He is walk'd up to the top of the hill: I'll go seek him.

He walked up to the top of the hill; I'll go and look for him.

[Retires.]

FAL.
I am accursed to rob in that thief's company:the rascal hath
removed my horse, and tied him I know not where. If I travel but
four foot by the squire further a-foot, I shall break my wind.
Well, I doubt not but to die a fair death for all this, if I 'scape
hanging for killing that rogue. I have forsworn his company hourly
any time this two-and-twenty year, and yet I am bewitch'd with the
rogue's company. If the rascal have not given me medicines to make
me love him, I'll be hang'd; it could not be else:I have drunk
medicines.--
Pointz!--Hal!--a plague upon you both!--Bardolph!--Peto!--I'll
starve, ere I'll rob a foot further. An 'twere not as good a deed as
drink, to turn true man, and to leave these rogues, I am the veriest
varlet that ever chewed with a tooth. Eight yards of uneven ground
is threescore and ten miles a-foot with me; and the stony-hearted
villains know it well enough:a plague upon't, when thieves cannot
be true one to another!
[They whistle.] Whew!--A plague upon you all! Give me
my horse, you rogues; give me my horse, and be hang'd!

*It's a curse to have to rob in that thief's company: the rascal has
taken my horse and I don't know where he's tied him up.If I
have to walk another four feet I'll be done for.
Well, I dare say I'll die a fair death for this, if I'm not
hanged for killing that rogue.Every hour of these past
twenty two years I've said I won't have any more to do with
him, but he seems to cast a spell over me.I'll be hanged if he
hasn't given me some potion to make me like him; it's the only explanation:
I have drunk medicines -
Pointz!Hal!Damn you both! Bardolph!Peto! I'll
starve before I do another robbery.And if it isn't as good a deed
as drinking to become a good man, and to leave these rogues,
I'm the greatest scoundrel alive.Eight yards over rough ground
is like a seventy mile walk for me; and the stony-hearted
villains know it well enough: curse the time, when thieves
have no loyalty to each other!
[Whistle] Whistling!Damn you all!Give me my horse, you scoundrels!
Give me my horse, and go hang yourselves!*

PRINCE.

[Coming forward.] Peace! lie down; lay thine ear close to the ground, and list if thou canst hear the tread of travellers.

Quiet! Lie down; put your ear to the ground
and listen for travellers.

FAL.
Have you any levers to lift me up again, being down? 'Sblood, I'll not bear mine own flesh so far a-foot again for all the coin in thy father's exchequer. What a plague mean ye to colt me thus?

Do you have levers to lift me up again once I'm down? By God,
I shan't walk so far on foot again, not for all the money in your
father's treasury. What the devil is this trick you're playing on me?

PRINCE.
Thou liest; thou art not colted, thou art uncolted.

You're lying; you're not tricked, you're unhorsed.

FAL.
I pr'ythee, good Prince Hal, help me to my horse, good king's son.

Please. good Prince Hal, help me find my horse, good king's
son.

PRINCE.
Out, ye rogue! shall I be your ostler?

Get lost, you rogue! Am I your groom?

FAL.
Go, hang thyself in thine own heir-apparent garters! If I be ta'en, I'll peach for this. An I have not ballads made on you all, and sung to filthy tunes, let a cup of sack be my poison. When a jest is so forward, and a-foot too, I hate it.

Go and hang yourself with your heir-apparent garters! If I'm caught
I'll turn informant. If I don't have songs written about you all,
and sung to filthy tunes, let me be poisoned with a cup of sack.
I hate this sort of practical joking, especially when it means I have to walk.

[Enter Gadshill.]

GADS.
Stand!

Stand!

FAL.
So I do, against my will.

I am, though I don't want to.

POINTZ.
O, 'tis our setter: I know his voice.

Oh, it's our informant; I know his voice.

[Comes forward with Bardolph and Peto.]

BARD.
What news?

What's the news?

GADS.
Case ye, case ye; on with your visards:there's money of the King's coming down the hill; 'tis going to the King's exchequer.

Hide yourselves, get your masks on: there's royal money coming down the hill; it's on its way to the King's treasury.

FAL.
You lie, ye rogue; 'tis going to the King's tavern.

You're lying, you scoundrel; it's going to the King's tavern.

GADS.
There's enough to make us all.

There's enough to make us all for life.

FAL.
To be hang'd.

To get us all hanged.

PRINCE.
Sirs, you four shall front them in the narrow lane; Ned Pointz and I will walk lower; if they 'scape from your encounter, then they light on us.

Gentlemen, you four will confront them in the narrow lane; Ned Pointz and I will walk round lower; if they escape you they'll run into us.

PETO.
How many be there of them?

How many of them are there?

GADS.
Some eight or ten.

About eight or ten.

FAL.
Zwounds, will they not rob us?

Good God, won't they rob us?

PRINCE.
What, a coward, Sir John Paunch?

What, are you a coward, Sir John Belly?

FAL.
Indeed, I am not John of Gaunt, your grandfather; but yet no coward, Hal.

It's true, I'm not John of Gaunt, your grandfather; but still, I'm not a coward, Hal.

PRINCE.
Well, we leave that to the proof.

Well, we'll wait and see.

POINTZ.
Sirrah Jack, thy horse stands behind the hedge:when thou
need'st him, there thou shalt find him. Farewell, and stand fast.

*Sir Jack, your horse is behind the hedge: when you need him,
that's where you'll find him.Farewell, and stand firm.*

FAL.
Now cannot I strike him, if I should be hang'd.

Now I can't strike him to save my life.

PRINCE.
[aside to POINTZ.] Ned, where are our disguises?

Ned, where are our disguises?

POINTZ.
[aside to PRINCE HENRY.] Here, hard by:stand close.

Here, close by; keep close to me.

[Exeunt Prince and Pointz.]

FAL.
Now, my masters, happy man be his dole, say I:every man
to his business.

*Now, my masters, may everyone be happy, I say; let everyone
go about his business.*

[Enter Travellers.]

FIRST TRAVELLER.
Come, neighbour:
The boy shall lead our horses down the hill;
We'll walk a-foot awhile and ease our legs.

*Come, neighbour:
the boy shall lead our horses down the hill;
we'll walk for a while to stretch our legs.*

FALS, GADS., &C.
Stand!

Stand!

SECOND TRAVELLER.
Jesu bless us!

Jesus bless us!

FAL.
Strike; down with them; cut the villains' throats. Ah,
whoreson caterpillars! bacon-fed knaves! they hate us youth:
down with them; fleece them.

Attack; knock them down; cut the villain's throats. Ah,
damned parasites! Greedy scoundrels! They hate we young people:
knock them down, clean them out.

FIRST TRAVELLER.
O, we're undone, both we and ours for ever!

Oh, we're lost, us and our descendants for ever!

FAL.
Hang ye, gorbellied knaves, are ye undone? No, ye fat chuffs;
I would your store were here! On, bacons on! What, ye knaves!
young men must live. You are grand-jurors, are ye? we'll jure
ye, i'faith.

Hang you, you potbellied knaves, are you lost? No, you fat swine;
I wish your foodstore was here! Go on, you pigs! What, you scoundrels!
Young men must live. Grand jurors are you? I swear we'll pass sentence
on you.

[Exeunt Fals., Gads., &c., driving the Travellers out.]

[Re-enter Prince Henry and Pointz, in buckram suits.]

PRINCE.
The thieves have bound the true men. Now, could thou and I rob
the thieves, and go merrily to London, it would be argument for a
week, laughter for a month, and a good jest for ever.

The thieves have caught the honest men. Now, if you and I can
rob the thieves, and go merrily to London, it would be gossip for a week,

cause laughter for a month, and be a good joke forever.

POINTZ.
Stand close:I hear them coming.

Come closer: I hear them coming.

[They retire.]

[Re-enter Falstaff, Gadshill, Bardolph, and Peto.]

FAL.
Come, my masters, let us share, and then to horse before day.
An the Prince and Pointz be not two arrant cowards, there's no
equity stirring:there's no more valour in that Pointz than in a
wild duck.

*Come, my masters, let's share out, and then get riding before daylight.
If the Prince and Pointz aren't two terrible cowards, I'm no judge:
there's no more bravery in Pointz than there is in a wild duck.*

[As they are sharing, the Prince and Poins set upon them.]

PRINCE.
Your money!

Give us your money!

POINTZ.
Villains!

Villains!

[Falstaff, after a blow or two, and the others run away, leaving
the booty behind them.]

PRINCE.
Got with much ease. Now merrily to horse:
The thieves are scatter'd, and possess'd with fear
So strongly that they dare not meet each other;
Each takes his fellow for an officer.
Away, good Ned. Fat Falstaff sweats to death,
And lards the lean earth as he walks along:
Were't not for laughing, I should pity him.

That was easily got.Now happily on to the horses:
the thieves are scattered, and so gripped with fear
that they dare not run into each other;
each one thinks the others are sherrifs.
Let's go, good Ned.Fat Falstaff is sweating to death,
he bastes the earth with grease as he goes:
if I wasn't laughing so much I'd feel sorry for him.

POINTZ.
How the rogue roar'd!

How the scoundrel screamed!

[Exeunt.]

Scene III. Warkworth.A Room in the Castle.

[Enter Hotspur, reading a letter.]

HOT.
--But, for mine own part, my lord, I could be well contented to
be there, in respect of the love I bear your House.--He could be
contented; why is he not, then? In respect of the love he bears
our House!--he shows in this, he loves his own barn better than he
loves our house. Let me see some more. The purpose you undertake
is dangerous;--Why, that's certain:'tis dangerous to take a cold,
to sleep, to drink; but I tell you, my lord fool, out of this nettle,
danger, we pluck this flower, safety. The purpose you undertake is
dangerous; the friends you have named uncertain; the time itself
unsorted; and your whole plot too light for the counterpoise of so
great an opposition.--
Say you so, say you so?I say unto you again, you are a shallow,
cowardly hind, and you lie. What a lack-brain is this! By the Lord,
our plot is a good plot as ever was laid; our friends true and
constant: a good plot, good friends, and full of expectation; an
excellent plot, very good friends. What a frosty-spirited rogue is
this! Why, my Lord of York commends the plot and the general course
of the action. Zwounds! an I were now by this rascal, I could brain
him with his lady's fan. Is there not my father, my uncle, and
myself? Lord Edmund Mortimer, my Lord of York, and Owen Glendower?
is there not, besides, the Douglas? have I not all their letters to
meet me in arms by the ninth of the next month? and are they not
some of them set forward already? What a pagan rascal is this! an
infidel! Ha! you shall see now, in very sincerity of fear and cold
heart, will he to the King, and lay open all our proceedings. O, I
could divide myself, and go to buffets, for moving such a dish of
skimm'd milk with so honourable an action!
Hang him! let him tell the King:we are prepared. I will set
forward to-night.--

[Enter Lady Percy.]

How now, Kate! I must leave you within these two hours.

" But for my part, my lord, I could be

very happy to be there, due to the love I have
for your family." He could be happy: then
why isn't he? Out of the love he has for our family: he
shows by this that he loves his own barn more than
he loves our house. Let me read some more. "The
action you plan is dangerous"–why, that's
obvious; it's dangerous to catch a cold, to sleep, to
drink; but I tell you, you foolish lord, out of this nettle of
danger we will pluck the flower of safety. "The action
you plan is dangerous, the friends you have named
are not reliable, the time is badly chosen and your
whole plot is too weak to combat the strength of
such a great enemy." That's what you say, is it? I say to
you again, you are a shallow cowardly fellow, and you
lie: what a lamebrain he is! By God, our plot is
a good plot, as good as was ever made, our friends true and
loyal: good plot, good friends, and excellent
chances: an excellent plot, very good friends; what a
cold spirited scoundrel this is! Why, my Lord of York
commends the plot, and the outline of the
plan. By God, if I were with this rascal now I
could beat his brains out with his lady's fan. Isn't there my
father, my uncle, and myself? Lord Edmund Mortimer,
my Lord of York, and Owen Glendower? Is
there not the Douglasses also? Had I had letters
from all of them saying they will meet me, armed, by the ninth of the next
month, and haven't some of them set out
already? What an unbelieving rascal this is, an infidel! Ha!
Now we'll see that in the depths of his fear and cold
feet he will go to the king, and reveal all our plans!
Oh, I could split myself in two and beat myself up,
for including such a milksop in our honourable
action! Hang him, let him tell the King, we
are prepared: I will set out tonight.

How are you, Kate? I must leave you within the next two hours.

LADY.
O, my good lord, why are you thus alone?
For what offence have I this fortnight been
A banish'd woman from my Harry's bed?
Tell me, sweet lord, what is't that takes from thee
Thy stomach, pleasure, and thy golden sleep?
Why dost thou bend thine eyes upon the earth,

And start so often when thou sitt'st alone?
Why hast thou lost the fresh blood in thy cheeks;
And given my treasures and my rights of thee
To thick-eyed musing and curst melancholy?
In thy faint slumbers I by thee have watch'd,
And heard thee murmur tales of iron wars;
Speak terms of manage to thy bounding steed;
Cry Courage! to the field! And thou hast talk'd
Of sallies and retires, of trenches, tents,
Of palisadoes, frontiers, parapets,
Of basilisks, of cannon, culverin,
Of prisoners ransomed, and of soldiers slain,
And all the 'currents of a heady fight.
Thy spirit within thee hath been so at war,
And thus hath so bestirr'd thee in thy sleep,
That beads of sweat have stood upon thy brow,
Like bubbles in a late-disturbed stream;
And in thy face strange motions have appear'd,
Such as we see when men restrain their breath
On some great sudden hest. O, what portents are these?
Some heavy business hath my lord in hand,
And I must know it, else he loves me not.

Oh my good Lord, why are you alone like this?
What have I done wrong to be banished from
my Harry's bed for the last fortnight?
Tell me, sweet Lord, what is it that has taken away
your appetite, your happiness and your ability to sleep?
Why are your eyes so downcast,
and why do you twitch so often when you're sitting alone?
Why are your cheeks so sickly and pale,
and why have you given up our marital pleasures
in exchange for ill tempered thinking and cursed melancholy?
I have been watching you in your restless sleep,
hearing you murmur stories of great wars,
talking as if you were riding your galloping horse,
crying "Courage! To battle!" And you have talked
of attacks, retreats, trenches, tents,
stakes, barriers, parapets,
all different sorts of cannon,
of ransoming prisoners, and dead soldiers,
and all the excitement of a great fight.
Your spirit has been so stirred up within you,
and has disturbed your sleep so much

that beads of sweat have appeared on your forehead
like bubbles in a recently disturbed stream,
and strange looks have appeared in your face,
as we see when men hold their breath
on receiving some great order. Oh, what do these signs mean?
My lord has some great affair in hand,
and he must tell me it, or he does not love me.

HOT.
What, ho!

[Enter a Servant.]

Is Gilliams with the packet gone?

Hello there!

Has Gilliams taken the messages?

SERV.
He is, my lord, an hour ago.

He has, my lord, an hour ago.

HOT.
Hath Butler brought those horses from the sheriff?

Has Butler bought those horses from the Sheriff?

SERV.
One horse, my lord, he brought even now.

He brought one horse, my lord, just a minute ago.

HOT.
What horse? a roan, a crop-ear, is it not?

What horse? A roan with notched ears, isn't it?

SERV.
It is, my lord.

It is, my lord.

HOT.
That roan shall be my throne.
Well, I will back him straight:O esperance!--
Bid Butler lead him forth into the park.

That's the one I shall ride.
Well, I will go straight to him: hope!
Tell Butler to take him out into the park.

[Exit Servant.]

LADY.
But hear you, my lord.

Just listen, my lord.

HOT.
What say'st thou, my lady?

What are you saying, my lady?

LADY.
What is it carries you away?

What is it that's taking you away?

HOT.
Why, my horse, my love, my horse.

Why, my horse, my love, my horse.

LADY.
Out, you mad-headed ape!
A weasel hath not such a deal of spleen
As you are toss'd with. In faith,
I'll know your business, Harry, that I will.
I fear my brother Mortimer doth stir
About his title, and hath sent for you
To line his enterprise:but if you go,--

Damn you, you mad headed ape!
A weasel isn't as quarrelsome
as you are. I swear,
I'll know what you're up to, Harry, I will;

I'm afraid my brother Mortimer is
planning to fight for his inheritance, and has sent for you
to back up his efforts: but if you go,–

HOT.
So far a-foot, I shall be weary, love.

So far on foot, I will be tired, love.

LADY.
Come, come, you paraquito, answer me
Directly to this question that I ask:
In faith, I'll break thy little finger, Harry,
An if thou wilt not tell me true.

Come, come, you parakeet, give me
a straight answer to my question:
I swear, I'll break your little finger, Harry,
if you don't tell me the truth.

HOT.
Away,
Away, you trifler! Love? I love thee not,
I care not for thee, Kate:this is no world
To play with mammets and to tilt with lips:
We must have bloody noses and crack'd crowns,
And pass them current too.--Gods me, my horse!--
What say'st thou, Kate? what wouldst thou have with me?

Go,
leave me alone, you lightweight! Love? I don't love you,
I don't care for you, Kate: this is no world
for playing with dolls, and to spend time kissing;
these times demand bloody noses and
broken crowns. God save me! My horse!
What are you saying, Kate? What do you want with me?

LADY.
Do you not love me? do you not indeed?
Well, do not, then; for, since you love me not,
I will not love myself. Do you not love me?
Nay, tell me if you speak in jest or no.

Don't you love me? Do you really not?

Well, then don't; for, since you don't love me,
I won't love myself. Don't you love me?
No, tell me if you're joking or not.

HOT.
Come, wilt thou see me ride?
And when I am o' horseback, I will swear
I love thee infinitely. But hark you, Kate;
I must not have you henceforth question me
Whither I go, nor reason whereabout:
Whither I must, I must; and, to conclude,
This evening must I leave you, gentle Kate.
I know you wise; but yet no further wise
Than Harry Percy's wife; constant you are;
But yet a woman:and, for secrecy,
No lady closer; for I well believe
Thou wilt not utter what thou dost not know;
And so far will I trust thee, gentle Kate.

Come, will you come and see me right?
When I'm on horseback, I will swear
that I love you infinitely. But listen, Kate;
from now on you must not question me
about where I'm going or what I'm doing:
I must go where I must go; and, in conclusion,
I must leave you this evening, gentle Kate.
I know you are wise; but no wiser
than Harry Percy's wife; you are loyal;
but you're still a woman: for keeping secrets,
there's no lady better; I certainly believe
you can't say what you don't know;
and this is as much as I'll trust you, sweet Kate.

LADY.
How! so far?

What! As much as that?

HOT.
Not an inch further. But hark you, Kate:
Whither I go, thither shall you go too;
To-day will I set forth, to-morrow you.
Will this content you, Kate?

Not an inch more. But listen, Kate:
wherever I go, you will go too;
today I will set out, tomorrow you.
Will this make you happy, Kate?

LADY.
It must of force.

I suppose it'll have to.

[Exeunt.]

Scene IV. Eastcheap. A Room in the Boar's-Head Tavern.

[Enter Prince Henry.]

PRINCE.
Ned, pr'ythee, come out of that fat room, and lend me thy
hand to laugh a little.

*Ned, come out of that stuffy room please, and lend me a
hand in laughing.*

[Enter Pointz.]

POINTZ.
Where hast been, Hal?

Where have you been, Hal?

PRINCE.
With three or four loggerheads amongst three or fourscore
hogsheads. I have sounded the very base-string of humility.
Sirrah, I am sworn brother to a leash of drawers; and can call
them all by their Christian names, as, Tom, Dick, and Francis.
They take it already upon their salvation, that though I be but
Prince of Wales, yet I am the king of courtesy; and tell me flatly
I am no proud Jack, like Falstaff, but a corinthian, a lad of mettle,
a good boy,--by the Lord, so they call me;--and, when I am King
of England, I shall command all the good lads in Eastcheap. They
call drinking deep, dying scarlet; and, when you breathe in your
watering, they hem! and bid you play it off. To conclude, I am
so good a proficient in one quarter of an hour, that I can drink with
any tinker in his own language during my life. I tell thee, Ned, thou
hast lost much honour, that thou wert not with me in this action. But,
sweet Ned,--to sweeten which name of Ned, I give thee this pennyworth
of sugar, clapp'd even now into my hand by an under-skinker; one that
never spake other English in his life than Eight shillings and sixpence,
and You are welcome; with this shrill addition, Anon, anon, sir! Score
a pint of bastard in the Half-moon,--or so.But, Ned, to drive away
the time till Falstaff come, I pr'ythee, do thou stand in some by-room,
while I question my puny drawer to what end he gave me the sugar;

and do thou never leave calling Francis! that his tale to me may be
nothing but Anon.Step aside, and I'll show thee a precedent.

With three or four blockheads, amongst three or
four score hogsheads. I have been with the lowest
of the low. Sir, I am now these sworn brother of a
trio of barmen, and can call them all by their
Christian names, Tom, Dick and Francis. They
swear upon their souls that although I'm
only Prince of Wales, I am the king of courtesy,
and they tell me straight that I am no proud fellow like Falstaff,
but a good companion, a feisty lad, a good boy (by God,
that's what they call me!), and when I am king of
England I will command all the good lads of Eastcheap.
They call heavy drinking "dying scarlet", and when
you have to stop your drinking to catch your breath they shout "cough!"
and order you to get on with your business. In conclusion, I have learned so much
in one quarter of an hour that I can now gossip with any gypsy in his own language.
I tell you, Ned, you certainly lost out by not being
with me for this engagement; but, sweet Ned–
to sweeten that name of Ned I'll give you this
pennyworth of sugar, slapped into my hand just now by
an under-barman, someone who never spoke any other English
in his life apart from "Eight shillings and sixpence", and
"You are welcome", with the shrill addition, "in a moment,
sir! Take a pint of Spanish wine to the Halfmoon room",
and so on. But Ned, to pass the time until Falstaff
comes:–I beg you to stand in some side room,
while I question my little barman as to why he
gave me the sugar, and you always keep on calling out
"Francis!" so that all he can say to me is
"In a minute". Step aside, and I'll show you how we'll do it.

[Exit Pointz.]

POINTZ.
[Within.]Francis!

Francis!

PRINCE.
Thou art perfect.

Perfect.

POINTZ.
[Within.]Francis!

Francis!

[Enter Francis.]

FRAN.
Anon, anon, sir.--Look down into the Pomegranate, Ralph.

In a minute, sir. Go and look in the Pomegranate room, Ralph.

PRINCE.
Come hither, Francis.

Come here, Francis.

FRAN.
My lord?

My lord?

PRINCE.
How long hast thou to serve, Francis?

How much of your apprenticeship have you left, Francis?

FRAN.
Forsooth, five years, and as much as to--

I swear, five years, and the same to–

POINTZ.
[within.] Francis!

Francis!

FRAN.
Anon, anon, sir.

In a minute, sir.

PRINCE.

Five year! by'r Lady, a long lease for the clinking of
pewter. But, Francis, darest thou be so valiant as to play
the coward with thy indenture and show it a fair pair of heels
and run from it?

Five years! By our Lady, that's a long time to learn
to serve drinks. But, Francis, are you so brave that you could
break your contract and show it a clean pair of heels
as you run from it?

FRAN.
O Lord, sir, I'll be sworn upon all the books in England,
I could find in my heart--

Oh lord, sir, I'll swear on all Bibles in England,
if I can find it in my heart–

POINTZ.
[within.] Francis!

Francis!

FRAN.
Anon, anon, sir.

In a minute, sir.

PRINCE.
How old art thou, Francis?

How old are you, Francis?

FRAN.
Let me see,--about Michaelmas next I shall be--

Let me see–at next Michaelmas I shall be–

POINTZ.
[within.] Francis!

Francis!

FRAN.
Anon, sir.--Pray you, stay a little, my lord.

In a minute, sir.–Excuse me, wait a little while, my lord.

PRINCE.
Nay, but hark you, Francis:for the sugar thou gavest
me, 'twas a pennyworth, was't not?

*No, but listen, Francis: that sugar you gave
me, it was a pennyworth, wasn't it?*

FRAN.
O Lord, sir, I would it had been two!

O Lord, Sir, I wish it had been two!

PRINCE.
I will give thee for it a thousand pound:ask me when
thou wilt, and thou shalt have it.

*I'll give you thousand pounds for it: ask me when you
want it, and you shall have it.*

POINTZ.
[within.] Francis!

Francis!

FRAN.
Anon, anon.

In a minute.

PRINCE.
Anon, Francis? No, Francis; but to-morrow, Francis; or,
Francis, a Thursday; or, indeed, Francis, when thou wilt. But,
Francis,--

*In a minute, Francis? No, Francis; but tomorrow, Francis; or,
Francis, on Thursday; or, indeed, Francis, when you want. But,
Francis–*

FRAN.
My lord?

My lord?

PRINCE.
--wilt thou rob this leathern-jerkin, crystal-button,
nott-pated, agate-ring, puke-stocking, caddis-garter,
smooth-tongue, Spanish-pouch,--

*–will you rob this leather jerkined, crystal buttoned,
cropped haired, agate ringed, bluestockinged, garter taped,
smooth tongued, leather pouched–*

FRAN.
O Lord, sir, who do you mean?

Oh Lord, Sir, who do you mean?

PRINCE.
Why, then, your brown bastard is your only drink; for,
look you, Francis, your white canvas doublet will sully:in
Barbary, sir, it cannot come to so much.

*Why, then, you'd better stick to serving wine; for,
Francis, if you rob your master you'll have to run for it:
your white coat won't stay too clean when you're on the run.*

FRAN.
What, sir?

What, sir?

POINTZ.
[within.] Francis!

Francis!

PRINCE.
Away, you rogue! dost thou not hear them call?

Off you go, you rogue! Can't you hear them calling?

[Here they both call him; Francis stands amazed, not knowing
which way to go.]

[Enter Vintner.]

VINT.
What, stand'st thou still, and hear'st such a calling? Look
to the guests within. [Exit Francis.]--My lord, old Sir John,
with half-a-dozen more, are at the door:shall I let them in?

What, are you standing here, when you can hear all this calling?
Go and look after the guests inside. My lord, old Sir John,
with half a dozen more, is at the door: shall I let them in?

PRINCE.
Let them alone awhile, and then open the door.

[Exit Vintner.]

Pointz!

Leave them out there for a while, and then open the door.
Pointz!

[Re-enter Pointz.]

POINTZ.
Anon, anon, sir.

In a minute, sir.

PRINCE.
Sirrah, Falstaff and the rest of the thieves are at the
door:shall we be merry?

Sir, Falstaff and the rest of the thieves are
outside: shall we have some fun?

POINTZ.
As merry as crickets, my lad. But hark ye; what cunning
match have you made with this jest of the drawer? Come,
what's the issue?

We'll be as merry as crickets, my lad.But listen, what's the big
idea with making fun of the barman like this?Come, what are you up to?

PRINCE.
I am now of all humours that have showed themselves humours

since the old days of goodman Adam to the pupil age of this
present twelve o'clock at midnight.--What's o'clock, Francis?

I'm in the mood to try every way of having fun ever
invented between good old Adam up to midnight
last night. – What's the time, Francis?

FRAN.
[Within.]Anon, anon, sir.

In a minute, sir.

PRINCE.
That ever this fellow should have fewer words than a parrot, and
yet the son of a woman! His industry is up-stairs and down-stairs;
his eloquence the parcel of a reckoning. I am not yet of Percy's
mind, the Hotspur of the North; he that kills me some six or seven
dozen of Scots at a breakfast, washes his hands, and says to his wife,
Fie upon this quiet life! I want work. O my sweet Harry, says she,
how many hast thoukill'd to-day?Give my roan horse a drench,
says he; and answers, Some fourteen, an hour after,--a trifle, a
trifle.
I pr'ythee, call in Falstaff:I'll play Percy, and that damn'd
brawn shall play Dame Mortimer his wife. Rivo! says the drunkard.
Call in ribs, call in tallow.

[Enter Falstaff, Gadshill, Bardolph, and Peto; followed by
Francis with wine.]

It's amazing that this fellow is a human being, when he has fewer
words than a parrot!All his efforts go into climbing the stairs,
his words are all to do with the bill.I don't share the mood of Percy,
the Hotspur of the north; the one who kills six or seven dozen
Scots at breakfast, washes his hands and says to his wife,
"Damn this quiet life!I want some work!" "Oh my sweet Harry," she says,
"How many have you killed today?" "Rinse down my roan horse,"
he says; and answers, "About fourteen, in an hour, nothing, nothing."

Please, call in Falstaff.I'll play Percy, and that great lout
shall play Lady Mortimer his wife.Cheers!
says the drunkard: call in these greedy devils.

POINTZ.
Welcome, Jack:where hast thou been?

Welcome, Jack: where have you been?

FAL.
A plague of all cowards, I say, and a vengeance too! marry, and
amen!--
Give me a cup of sack, boy.--Ere I lead this life long, I'll sew
nether-stocks, and mend them and foot them too. A plague of all
cowards!--
Give me a cup of sack, rogue.--Is there no virtue extant?

*Damn all cowards, I say, and revenge on them too!Yes, amen
to that!
Give me a cup of sack, boy.I'd rather sew stockings and mend them
than live this life.Damnation to all cowards!
Give me a cup of sack, scoundrel.Are there no good men left?*

[Drinks.]

PRINCE.
Didst thou never see Titan kiss a dish of butter? pitiful-hearted
butter, that melted at the sweet tale of the Sun! if thou didst,
then behold that compound.

*Didn't you ever see the sun shining on a dish of butter?Soft
hearted butter, that melted at a touch of the sun!If you did,
you can see it in front of you here.*

FAL.
You rogue, here's lime in this sack too:there is nothing but roguery
to be found in villainous man:yet a coward is worse than a cup of
sack with lime in it, a villanous coward.--Go thy ways, old Jack:die
when thou wilt, if manhood, good manhood, be not forgot upon the face
of the Earth, then am I a shotten herring. There live not three good
men unhang'd in England; and one of them is fat, and grows old: God
help the while! a bad world, I say.
I would I were a weaver; I could sing psalms or any thing. A plague of
all cowards! I say still.

*You rogue, there's lime in this sack as well: all one finds in villainous mankind
is roguery: but a coward is worse than a cup of sack with lime in it,
a villainous coward – go about your business, old Jack: whenever
you die, if manhood, good manhood, hasn't vanished
from the face of the earth then I'm a dried up herring.There aren't three good*

men left unhanged in England, and one of them is old and fat, God help us,
it's a bad world, I say. I wish I was a weaver; I could sing psalms,
or anything. I still say, damnation to all cowards.

PRINCE.
How now, wool-sack? what mutter you?

What's this, wool sack? What are you muttering about?

FAL.
A king's son! If I do not beat thee out of thy kingdom with a dagger
of lath, and drive all thy subjects afore thee like a flock of
wild-geese, I'll never wear hair on my face more. You Prince of Wales!

A king's son! If I don't drive you out of your kingdom with a wooden
dagger, with all your subjects running ahead like a flock
of wild geese, I'll cut my beard off. You, Prince of Wales!

PRINCE.
Why, you whoreson round man, what's the matter?

Why, you round old son of a bitch, what's the matter?

FAL.
Are not you a coward? answer me to that:--and Pointz there?

Aren't you a coward? Answer me that: and Pointz there?

POINTZ.
Zwounds, ye fat paunch, an ye call me coward, by the Lord, I'll
stab thee.

By heaven, you great fatty, if you call me a coward, by God
I'll stab you.

FAL.
I call thee coward! I'll see thee damn'd ere I call thee coward:
but I would give a thousand pound, I could run as fast as thou canst.
You are straight enough in the shoulders; you care not who sees your
back: call you that backing of your friends? A plague upon such
backing! give me them that will face me.--Give me a cup of sack:
I am a rogue, if I drunk to-day.

I, call you a coward! I'll see you damned before I call you a coward:

but I would give a thousand pounds, to be able to run as fast as you.
Your shoulders are straight enough; you don't care who sees your
back: do you call that supporting your friends? Damn such supporters!
Give me ones who'll face me. – Give me a cup of sack:
I'm a rogue if I've had a drink yet today.

PRINCE.
O villain! thy lips are scarce wiped since thou drunk'st last.

You villain! You've hardly wiped the last drink off your lips!

FAL.
All is one for that. A plague of all cowards! still say I.

Whatever. Damn all cowards, I still say!

[Drinks.]

PRINCE.
What's the matter?

What's the matter?

FAL.
What's the matter? there be four of us here have ta'en a thousand
pound this day morning.

What's the matter? Four of us here stole a thousand
pounds this morning.

PRINCE.
Where is it, Jack? where is it?

Where is it, Jack, where is it?

FAL.
Where is it! taken from us it is:a hundred upon poor four of us!

Where is it! Taken from us, a hundred setting on we poor four!

PRINCE.
What, a hundred, man?

What, a hundred of them, man?

FAL.
I am a rogue, if I were not at half-sword with a dozen of them two
hours together. I have 'scaped by miracle. I am eight times thrust
through the doublet, four through the hose; my buckler cut through
and through; my sword hack'd like a hand-saw,--ecce signum! I never
dealt better since I was a man:all would not do. A plague of all
cowards! Let them speak:if they speak more or less than truth,
they are villains and the sons of darkness.

I'm a scoundrel, if I wasn't in close combat with a dozen of them
for two hours at a stretch.I escaped by a miracle.I've taken eight
stabs through my jacket, four through my stockings, my belt has been
chopped to pieces, my sword is notched like a handsaw-
there's the proof!I never fought better in my life:
not everyone could have done that!Damn all cowards!
Let them explain themselves, and if they say more or less
than the truth, they are villains and devils.

PRINCE.
Speak, sirs; how was it?

Speak, sirs; what happened?

GADS.
We four set upon some dozen,--

We four set on a dozen men –

FAL.
Sixteen at least, my lord.

Sixteen at least, my lord.

GADS.
--and bound them.

And tied them up.

PETO.
No, no; they were not bound.

No, they weren't tied.

FAL.

You rogue, they were bound, every man of them; or I am a Jew else, an Ebrew Jew.

You scoundrel, they were tied up, every one of them; otherwise I'm a Jew, a Jewish Jew.

GADS.

As we were sharing, some six or seven fresh men set upon us,--

As we were sharing out the money, six or seven new men set on us-

FAL.

And unbound the rest, and then come in the other.

And untied the rest, who then joined in with them.

PRINCE.

What, fought you with them all?

What, did you fight them all?

FAL.

All? I know not what you call all; but if I fought not with fifty of them, I am a bunch of radish:if there were not two or three and fifty upon poor old Jack, then am I no two-legged creature.

All?I don't know what you mean by all; but if I didn't fight fifty of them, I'm a bunch of radishes: If there weren't fifty-two or three on poor old Jack, I'm not a man.

PRINCE.

Pray God you have not murdered some of them.

I pray to God you didn't murder any of them.

FAL.

Nay, that's past praying for: I have pepper'd two of them; two I am sure I have paid, two rogues in buckram suits. I tell thee what, Hal, if I tell thee a lie, spit in my face, call me horse. Thou knowest my old ward:here I lay, and thus I bore my point. Four rogues in buckram let drive at me,--

No good praying for that: I've drilled holes in two of them; I'm sure

I killed two, two rogues in canvas overalls.I tell you what,
Hal, if I tell you a lie, spit in my face and call me a horse.
You know how I stand in a fight: this was my guard, and I thrust like this.
Four scoundrels in canvas suits set on me –

PRINCE.
What, four? thou saidst but two even now.

What, four?It was two just now.

FAL.
Four, Hal; I told thee four.

Four, Hal; I said four.

POINTZ.
Ay, ay, he said four.

Yes, yes, he said four.

FAL.
These four came all a-front, and mainly thrust at me. I made me no more
ado but took all their seven points in my target, thus.

These four attacked me from the front, and attacked me strongly.I didn't
mess about but fended off all seven swords with my shield, like this.

PRINCE.
Seven? why, there were but four even now.

Seven?What, there were only four just now.

FAL.
In buckram?

In canvas?

POINTZ.
Ay, four, in buckram suits.

Yes, four, in canvas overalls.

FAL.
Seven, by these hilts, or I am a villain else.

Seven, I swear on my sword, or I'm a villain.

PRINCE.
[aside to Pointz.] Pr'ythee let him alone; we shall have more anon.

Let him run on; there'll be more of them soon.

FAL.
Dost thou hear me, Hal?

Are you listening, Hal?

PRINCE.
Ay, and mark thee too, Jack.

Yes, and noting what you say, Jack.

FAL.
Do so, for it is worth the listening to. These nine in buckram that I told thee of,--

*Do, for it's worth listening to. These nine in canvas
I told you about-*

PRINCE.
So, two more already.

So, two more already.

FAL.
--their points being broken,--

With their swords broken –

POINTZ.
Down fell their hose.

Their drawers fell down.

FAL.
--began to give me ground:but I followed me close, came in foot and hand; and with a thought seven of the eleven I paid.

84

*they began to retreat; but I followed them close, pressing
them hand and foot; and quick as thinking I finished off seven of eleven.*

PRINCE.

O monstrous! eleven buckram men grown out of two!

How monstrous, eleven canvas clad men grown from two!

FAL.

But, as the Devil would have it, three misbegotten knaves in Kendal
Green came at my back and let drive at me; for it was so dark, Hal,
that thou couldst not see thy hand.

*But, as the Devil planned, three bastard knaves in camouflage
came up behind and attacked me; for it was so dark, Hal, one
couldn't see one's own hand.*

PRINCE.

These lies are like the father that begets them, gross as a mountain,
open, palpable. Why, thou nott-pated fool, thou whoreson, obscene
greasy tallow-keech,--

*These lies are like the one who creates them, big as a mountain,
obvious, clear.Why, you blockhead, you son of a bitch, obscene
mound of candle-fat-*

FAL.

What, art thou mad? art thou mad? is not the truth the truth?

What, are you mad, are you mad?Isn't the truth the truth?

PRINCE.

Why, how couldst thou know these men in Kendal green, when it was
so dark thou couldst not see thy hand? come, tell us your reason:
what sayest thou to this?

*Well, how could you see these men on camouflage, when it was
so dark you couldn't see your hand?Come on, tell us your reason:
what have you got to say to that?*

POINTZ.

Come, your reason, Jack, your reason.

Come, your reason, Jack, your reason.

FAL.
What, upon compulsion? No; were I at the strappado, or all the racks
in the world, I would not tell you on compulsion. Give you a reason on
compulsion! if reasons were as plentiful as blackberries, I would
give no man a reason upon compulsion, I.

*What, because you demand it? No, if I was given the worst torture
in the world, I won't do as you order me. Give you explanations on
orders! If explanations were as plentiful as blackberries, I wouldn't give
any man an explanation under duress.*

PRINCE.
I'll be no longer guilty of this sin; this sanguine coward, this
bed-presser, this horse-back-breaker, this huge hill of flesh,--

*I'll no longer be guilty of this sin; this boozy coward, this
bed presser, this breaker of horses' backs, this great hill of flesh-*

FAL.
Away, you starveling, you eel-skin, you dried neat's-tongue, you
stock-fish,--
O, for breath to utter what is like thee!--you tailor's-yard, you
sheath, you bow-case, you vile standing tuck,--

*Get lost, you famished eelskin, you dried oxtongue, you
dried cod –
Oh, I wish I had the breath to say what you're like! You
piece of cloth, you scabbard, you bow-case, you broken sword -*

PRINCE.
Well, breathe awhile, and then to it again: and, when thou hast
tired thyself in base comparisons, hear me speak but this:--

*Well, pause for breath and then carry on: and, when you have
worn yourself out with low comparisons, let me tell you this:*

POINTZ.
Mark, Jack.

Take a note of this, Jack.

PRINCE.

--We two saw you four set on four; you bound them, and were masters of
their wealth.--Mark now, how a plain tale shall put you down.--
Then did we two set on you four; and, with a word, outfaced you from
your prize, and have it; yea, and can show it you here in the house:
and, Falstaff, you carried yourself away as nimbly, with as quick
dexterity, and roared for mercy, and still ran and roar'd, as ever I
heard bull-calf. What a slave art thou, to hack thy sword as thou
hast done, and then say it was in fight!
What trick, what device, what starting-hole canst thou now find
out to hide thee from this open and apparent shame?

*We two saw you four attack four; you tied them up, and had
their money. – Now see how a simple tale will knock you back –
Then we two set on you four; and, with a word, scared you off
your prize, and we have it; yes, we can show it to you here in this house:
and, Falstaff, you ran away as nimbly, with as much agility,
such roaring for mercy, and you still ran and roared, as any
bull-calf I ever heard.What a slave you are, to hack up your sword
as you have, and then say you were in a fight!
What trick, what cover, what hiding place can you now find
to hide you from this open and obvious shame?*

POINTZ.
Come, let's hear, Jack; what trick hast thou now?

Come, let's hear it, Jack; what trick have you got now?

FAL.
By the Lord, I knew ye as well as he that made ye. Why, hear ye,
my masters:
Was it for me to kill the heir-apparent? should I turn upon the
true Prince? why, thou knowest I am as valiant as Hercules:but
beware instinct; the lion will not touch the true Prince.
Instinct is a great matter; I was now a coward on instinct.
I shall think the better of myself and thee during my life; I for a
valiant lion, and thou for a true prince.But, by the Lord, lads,
I am glad you have the money.--
[To Hostess within.]Hostess, clap-to the doors:watch
to-night, pray to-morrow.--Gallants, lads, boys, hearts of gold,
all the titles of good fellowship come to you!
What, shall we be merry? shall we have a play extempore?

*By the Lord, I recognized you as well as your own fathers would.Why, listen,
my masters:*

should I have killed the heir-apparent?Should I attack the
true Prince?Why, you know I am as brave as Hercules: but
look out for instinct; a lion won't touch a true Prince.
Instinct is very powerful.I was a coward by instinct: I will think better of myself now,
and you – I'm a brave lion, and you are a true prince.But, by heaven, lads,
I'm glad you have the money.Hostess, slam the doors!Party tonight, pray tomorrow! Brave lads,
boys, hearts of gold, all good fellowship to you!
What, shall we be merry, shall we put on a show?

PRINCE.
Content; and the argument shall be thy running away.

Why not, and the plot will be you running away.

FAL.
Ah, no more of that, Hal, an thou lovest me!

Ah, no more of that, Hal, if you love me!

[Enter the Hostess.]

HOST.
O Jesu, my lord the Prince,--

Oh Jesus, my lord the Prince-

PRINCE.
How now, my lady the hostess! What say'st thou to me?

Hello there, my landlady!What are you telling me?

HOST.
Marry, my lord, there is a nobleman of the Court at door would
speak with you: he says he comes from your father.

*Well, my lord, there is a nobleman from the Court at the door
who wants to speak to you: he says he's come from your father.*

PRINCE.
Give him as much as will make him a royal man, and send him back
again to my mother.

*Tip him a suitable sum for royalties, and send him back
to my mother.*

FAL.
What manner of man is he?

What sort of man is he?

HOST.
An old man.

An old man.

FAL.
What doth gravity out of his bed at midnight? Shall I give him
his answer?

*What is an old man doing out of bed at midnight? Shall I
tell him where to go?*

PRINCE.
Pr'ythee, do, Jack.

Please do, Jack.

FAL.
Faith, and I'll send him packing.

By God, I'll send him packing.

[Exit.]

PRINCE.
Now, sirs:--by'r Lady, you fought fair;--so did you, Peto;--so did you,
Bardolph:you are lions, too, you ran away upon instinct, you will not
touch the true Prince; no,--fie!

*Now, gentlemen – by the Lady, you fought well – so did you, Peto; so did you,
Bardolph: you are lions, too, you ran away on instinct, you wouldn't
touch the true Prince, no – rubbish!*

BARD.
Faith, I ran when I saw others run.

I swear, I ran because the others did.

PRINCE.
Tell me now in earnest, how came Falstaff's sword so hack'd?

Now tell me truthfully, how did Falstaff's sword get so damaged?

PETO.
Why, he hack'd it with his dagger; and said he would swear truth out of
England, but he would make you believe it was done in fight; and
persuaded us to do the like.

*Why, he hacked it with his dagger; and he said he would tell any lie
he had to, but he would make you believe it was done in a fight; and
he persuaded us to do the same.*

BARD.
Yea, and to tickle our noses with spear-grass to make them bleed;
and then to beslubber our garments with it, and swear it was the
blood of true men. I did that I did not this seven year before;
I blush'd to hear his monstrous devices.

*Yes, and to stick sharp grasses up our noses to make them bleed;
and then to smear our clothes with it, and swear it was the
blood of brave men.I did something I haven't done for the last seven years;
I blushed to hear his plans.*

PRINCE.
O villain, thou stolest a cup of sack eighteen years ago, and wert
taken with the manner, and ever since thou hast blush'd extempore.
Thou hadst fire and sword on thy side, and yet thou rann'st away:
what instinct hadst thou for it?

*Oh villain, you stole a cup of sack eighteen years ago, and
got a taste for it, and ever since then you can blush at will.
You had numbers and weapons on your side, but you ran away;
what's your excuse?*

BARD.
My lord, do you see these meteors? do you behold these
exhalations?

My lord, do you see these fiery meteors?

PRINCE.
I do.

I do.

BARD.
What think you they portend?

What do you think they predict?

PRINCE.
Hot livers and cold purses.

Hot livers and empty purses.

BARD.
Choler, my lord, if rightly taken.

Anger, my lord, if correctly taken.

PRINCE.
No, if rightly taken, halter.--Here comes lean Jack, here comes
bare-bone.--

[Enter Falstaff.]

How now, my sweet creature of bombast! How long is't ago, Jack,
since thou saw'st thine own knee?

*No, arrests, if you get properly taken. Here comes skinny Jack, here comes
the skeleton –*

*Hello there, my old pile of stuffing! How long ago is it, Jack,
since you saw your own knees?*

FAL.
My own knee! when I was about thy years, Hal, I was not an eagle's
talon in the waist; I could have crept into any alderman's thumb-ring:
a plague of sighing and grief! it blows a man up like a bladder.
There's villanous news abroad: here was Sir John Bracy from your
father; you must to the Court in the morning.
That same mad fellow of the North, Percy; and he of Wales, that gave
Amaimon the bastinado, and swore the Devil his true liegeman upon the
cross of a Welsh hook,--what a plague call you him?

My own knees! When I was about your age, Hal, an eagle could have

got its claw round my waist; I could have crept in through an alderman's thumb ring:
it's all this sighing and grief! It blows a man up like a bladder.
There's bad news outside: that was Sir John Bracy from your
father; you must go to court in the morning.
That madman in the North, Percy; he and that Welshman, who
gave a demon a beating, and swore the Devil was his ally on
a blasphemous Welsh cross – what the hell's his name?

POINTZ.
O, Glendower.

Oh, Glendower.

FAL.
Owen, Owen,--the same; and his son-in-law Mortimer; and old
Northumberland; and that sprightly Scot of Scots, Douglas, that
runs o' horseback up a hill perpendicular,--

Owen, Owen, that's the one; and his son-in-law Mortimer; and old
Northumberland; and that active Scot, Douglas, who
can ride his horse up a sheer hillside-

PRINCE.
He that rides at high speed and with his pistol kills a sparrow
flying.

The one who can kill a sparrow in flight with a pistol whilst
galloping at high speed.

FAL.
You have hit it.

You've hit it.

PRINCE.
So did he never the sparrow.

And he never hit the sparrow.

FAL.
Well, that rascal hath good metal in him; he will not run.

Well, that rascal has a good temperament; he won't run.

PRINCE.

Why, what a rascal art thou, then, to praise him so for running!

Why, what a rascal you are, then, to praise him for running like that!

FAL.

O' horseback, ye cuckoo! but a-foot he will not budge a foot.

On horseback, you fool! But on the ground he won't budge.

PRINCE.

Yes, Jack, upon instinct.

Yes Jack, on instinct.

FAL.

I grant ye, upon instinct. Well, he is there too, and one Mordake,
and a thousand blue-caps more:
Worcester is stolen away to-night; thy father's beard is turn'd
white with the news:you may buy land now as cheap as stinking
mackerel.

*I'll give you that, on instinct. Well, he's there too, and someone called Mordrake,
and a thousand Scottish blue-bonnets as well:
Worcester sneaked away this evening; your father's beard has turned
white with the news: you can buy land now as cheap as rotten mackrel.*

PRINCE.

Why then, it is like if there came a hot June, and
this civil buffeting hold, we shall buy maidenheads
as they buy hobnails, by the hundreds.

*Well then, it's as if it's a hot June, and if this
civil strife carries on none of the girls will
be able to resist us, they'll be two a penny.*

FAL.

But, tell me, Hal, art not thou horrible afeard? thou being
heir-apparent, could the world pick thee out three such enemies again
as that fiend Douglas, that spirit Percy, and that devil Glendower?
art thou not horribly afraid? doth not thy blood thrill at it?

*But tell me, Hal, aren't you terribly afraid? Being
heir-apparent, could you find three worse enemies in the world*

as that demon Douglas, that ghost Percy, and that devil Glendower?
Aren't you terribly afraid?Doesn't it make your blood run cold?

PRINCE.
Not a whit, i'faith; I lack some of thy instinct.

Not at all, I swear; I don't have your instinct.

FAL.
Well, thou wilt be horribly chid to-morrow when thou comest to
thy father.If thou love life, practise an answer.

Well, you're going to get an awful telling off tomorrow when
you see your father.If you love life, have an answer ready.

PRINCE.
Do thou stand for my father and examine me upon the particulars
of my life.

You stand in for my father and question me about
my lifestyle.

FAL.
Shall I? content:this chair shall be my state, this dagger my
sceptre, and this cushion my crown.

Shall I?Alright: this chair is my throne, this dagger my sceptre,
and this cushion my crown.

PRINCE.
Thy state is taken for a joint-stool, thy golden sceptre for a
leaden dagger, and thy precious rich crown for a pitiful bald crown.

So we have a wooden stool for your throne, a lead dagger for your
golden sceptre, and a sad bald head for a golden crown.

FAL.
Well, an the fire of grace be not quite out of thee, now shalt
thou be moved.--
Give me a cup of sack, to make my eyes look red, that it may be
thought I have wept; for I must speak in passion, and I will do it
in King Cambyses' vein.

Well, if you have any grace left in you, you will

be moved.-
Give me a cup of sack, to make my eyes look red, so it looks
as if I've been weeping; for I must speak with passion, and I will
imitate King Cambyses.

PRINCE.
Well, here is my leg.

Well, I kneel to you.

FAL.
And here is my speech.--Stand aside, nobility.

And here's what I say. – Stand back, noblemen.

HOST.
O Jesu, this is excellent sport, i faith!

Oh Jesus, I swear this is good fun!

FAL.
Weep not, sweet Queen; for trickling tears are vain.

Do not weep, sweet queen; trickling tears are useless.

HOST.
O, the Father, how he holds his countenance!

Oh, by God, how does he keep a straight face!

FAL.
For God's sake, lords, convey my tristful Queen;
For tears do stop the floodgates of her eyes.

For God's sake, lords, take my sad Queen away;
tears are blocking the floodgates of her eyes.

HOST.
O Jesu, he doth it as like one of these harlotry players as ever
I see!

Oh Jesus, he's as good as any of those rascal actors!

FAL.

Peace, good pint-pot; peace, good tickle-brain.--Harry, I do not
only marvel where thou spendest thy time, but also how thou art
accompanied:for though the camomile, the more it is trodden on,
the faster it grows, yet youth, the more it is wasted, the sooner
it wears. That thou art my son, I have partly thy mother's word,
partly my own opinion; but chiefly a villainous trick of thine eye,
and a foolish hanging of thy nether lip, that doth warrant me. If,
then, thou be son to me, here lies the point:Why, being son to me,
art thou so pointed at?
Shall the blessed Sun of heaven prove a micher, and eat blackberries?
a question not to be ask'd. Shall the son of England prove a thief,
and take purses? a question to be ask'd.
There is a thing, Harry, which thou hast often heard of, and it is
known to many in our land by the name of pitch:this pitch, as
ancient writers do report, doth defile; so doth the company thou
keepest:for, Harry, now I do not speak to thee in drink, but in
tears; not in pleasure, but in passion; not in words only,
but in woes also.And yet there is a virtuous man whom I have
often noted in thy company, but I know not his name.

Quiet, pint-pot, quiet, booze-brain.-
Harry, I don't only wonder where you've been spending your time,
but also who you hang around with.For though
chamomile grows better the more you trample it,
the more you spend your youth the quicker you lose it.
I have partly your mother's word that you are my son,
partly my own opinion, but mainly a villainous trick of your eye, and the foolish
droop of your lower lip, that gives me proof. If
then you are my son, here's the point – why,
if you're my son, do you get so pointed at?Shall the
blessed sun of heaven be a truant, off blackberrying?
It's out of the question.Shall the
sun of England prove to be a thief, and steal purses? A
question we must ask.There's a thing, Harry, which
you will often have heard of, and many in our country
call it pitch.This pitch (as ancient writers tell us) defiles,
and so does the company you keep; for, Harry, I'm not
talking through drink, but through tears; not in happiness, but passion,
not only through my words but through my sorrow.
But there is a good man whom I have often seen
in your company, though I do not know his name.

PRINCE.
What manner of man, an it like your Majesty?

What sort of man, if you please, your Majesty?

FAL.
A goodly portly man, i'faith, and a corpulent; of a cheerful look,
a pleasing eye, and a most noble carriage; and, as I think, his age
some fifty, or, by'r Lady, inclining to threescore; and now I
remember me, his name is Falstaff:if that man should be lewdly given,
he deceiveth me; for, Harry, I see virtue in his looks.
If, then, the tree may be known by the fruit, as the fruit by the tree,
then, peremptorily I speak it, there is virtue in that Falstaff:him
keep with, the rest banish. And tell me now, thou naughty varlet, tell
me where hast thou been this month?

*A good dignified man, I swear, a full bodied one; with a cheerful look,
an attractive eye, and a very noble bearing; his age, I think, about
fifty, or, maybe, getting on for sixty; and now I
remember, his name is Falstaff:if that man has vulgar inclinations
he's fooled me; for, Harry, I can see virtue in his looks.
If, then, the tree can be judged by its fruit, as the fruit by the tree,
then I say confidently that there is virtue in that Falstaff: keep him,
send the rest away.And now, tell me, you naughty scoundrel, tell
me where you have been the last month?*

PRINCE.
Dost thou speak like a king? Do thou stand for me, and I'll play
my father.

*Are you talking like a king?You play me, and I'll
play your father.*

FAL.
Depose me! if thou dost it half so gravely, so majestically, both
in word and matter, hang me up by the heels for a rabbit-sucker or a
poulter's hare.

*Overthrow me! If you do it with half as much dignity and majesty,
hang me up as a skinny rabbit or a hare in a poulterer's.*

PRINCE.
Well, here I am set.

Well, here I sit.

FAL.
And here I stand.--Judge, my masters.

And here I stand – Judge it, my masters.

PRINCE.
Now, Harry, whence come you?

Now, Harry, where have you come from?

FAL.
My noble lord, from Eastcheap.

My noble lord, from Eastcheap.

PRINCE.
The complaints I hear of thee are grievous.

I've heard many bad things said about you.

FAL.
'Sblood, my lord, they are false.--Nay, I'll tickle ye for a
young prince, i'faith.

*By God, my lord, it's not true – I'll make you laugh at
my impression of a young prince, I swear.*

PRINCE.
Swearest thou, ungracious boy? henceforth ne'er look on me. Thou art
violently carried away from grace:there is a devil haunts thee, in
the likeness of an old fat man,--a tun of man is thy companion. Why
dost thou converse with that trunk of humours, that bolting-hutch of
beastliness, that swollen parcel of dropsies, that huge bombard of
sack, that roasted Manningtree ox with the pudding in his belly, that
reverend Vice, that grey Iniquity, that father ruffian, that vanity
in years? Wherein is he good, but to taste sack and drink it? wherein
neat and cleanly, but to carve a capon and eat it? wherein cunning, but
in craft? wherein crafty, but in villany? wherein villainous, but in
all things? wherein worthy, but in nothing?

*You swear, graceless boy? From now on don't come near me. You are
violently removed from grace: there is a devil who haunts you, in
the shape of a fat old man–a barrel of a man who is your companion. Why
do you associate with that trunk of diseases, that bin full of beastliness,*

that great parcel of swellings, that huge wine bag of
sack, that roasted Manningtree ox with pudding in his belly, that
old Vice, that grey Iniquity, that fatherly ruffian, that aged vanity?
What's he good for, except for tasting and drinking sack? What
can he do neatly and cleanly, except for carving a chicken and eating it?
How is he skilful, except for cheating? What's he do with that, except being a villain? What's he
villainous at, except everything? What is he good at,
apart from nothing?

FAL.
I would your Grace would take me with you:whom means your Grace?

I wish I understood what your Grace's saying: whom does your Grace mean?

PRINCE.
That villainous abominable misleader of youth, Falstaff, that old
white-bearded Satan.

That villainous abominable misleader of youth, Falstaff, that old
white bearded devil.

FAL.
My lord, the man I know.

My Lord, I know the man.

PRINCE.
I know thou dost.

I know you do.

FAL.
But to say I know more harm in him than in myself, were to say more
than I know. That he is old,--(the more the pity,--his white hairs do
witness it. If sack and sugar be a fault, God help the wicked! if to
be old and merry be a sin, then many an old host that I know is damn'd:
if to be fat be to be hated, then Pharaoh's lean kine are to be loved.
No, my good lord:banish Peto, banish Bardolph, banish Pointz; but,
for sweet Jack Falstaff, kind Jack Falstaff, true Jack Falstaff,
valiant Jack Falstaff, and therefore more valiant, being, as he is, old
Jack Falstaff, banish not him thy Harry's company, banish not him thy
Harry's company:banish plump Jack, and banish all the world.

But I can't say that there is any more harm in him than there is in

myself. That he is old—more's the pity—is shown by his white hairs.
If liking sack and sugar is a fault, God help wicked people! If to
be old and merry is a sin, then many old landlords I know are going to hell:
if one should be hated for being fat, then Pharaoh's thin cattle should be loved.
No, my good lord: banish Peto, banish Bardolph, banish Pointz; but,
as for sweet Jack Falstaff, kind Jack Falstaff, true Jack Falstaff,
brave Jack Falstaff, who is even more brave because he is old
Jack Falstaff, don't forbid your Harry to have him for company, don't forbid him:
if you banish plump Jack, you banish the whole world.

PRINCE.
I do, I will.

I do, and I will.

[A knocking heard.]

[Exeunt Hostess, Francis, and Bardolph.]

[Enter Bardolph, running.]

BARD.
O, my lord, my lord! the sheriff with a most monstrous watch is
at the door.

Oh my lord, my lord! The Sheriff is at the door with a
great force of men.

FAL.
Out, ye rogue!--Play out the play:I have much to say in the
behalf of that Falstaff.

Get out, you scoundrel! Let's carry on with the play: I have a lot to say in the
defence of that Falstaff.

[Re-enter the Hostess, hastily.]

HOST.
O Jesu, my lord, my lord,--

O Jesus, my lord, my lord,–

Prince.
Heigh, heigh! the Devil rides upon a fiddlestick:what's the matter?

Hello! the devil is leading the dance: what's the matter?

Host.
The sheriff and all the watch are at the door:they are come to
search the house. Shall I let them in?

*The sheriff and all the watch are at the door: they have come to
search the house. Shall I let them in?*

FAL.
Dost thou hear, Hal? Never call a true piece of gold a counterfeit:
thou art essentially made without seeming so.

*Did you hear that, Hal? Don't tell them a good man like me is bad:
you have all the good qualities, but you don't show them.*

Prince.
And thou a natural coward, without instinct.

And you are natural coward, with no instinct.

FAL.
I deny your major:if you will deny the sheriff, so; if not, let him
enter:if I become not a cart as well as another man, a plague on my
bringing up! I hope I shall as soon be strangled with a halter as
another.

*I reject your thesis: if you will reject the Sheriff, good; if not, let him
come in: if I don't look as good on a tumbril as the next man,
a plague on my upbringing! I think I'll make just as good a victim
for the hangman as another.*

PRINCE.
Go, hide thee behind the arras:--the rest walk, up above.Now,
my masters, for a true face and good conscience.

*Go, hide yourself behind the curtain: the rest of you go upstairs. Now,
my masters, I need an honest face and a good conscience.*

FAL.
Both which I have had; but their date is out, and therefore I'll
hide me.

I've had both in the past; but they are past their sell by date, and so I'll hide.

PRINCE.
Call in the sheriff.--

[Exeunt all but the Prince and Pointz.]

[Enter Sheriff and Carrier.]

Now, master sheriff, what's your will with me?

Call in the Sheriff.

Now, Master Sheriff, what do you want with me?

SHER.
First, pardon me, my lord. A hue-and-cry
Hath followed certain men unto this house.

*Firstly, forgive me, my lord. A hue and cry
has followed certain men to this house.*

PRINCE.
What men?

What men?

SHER.
One of them is well known, my gracious lord,--
A gross fat man.

*One of them is well known, my gracious lord–
a grotesquely fat man.*

CAR.
As fat as butter.

As fat as butter.

PRINCE.
The man, I do assure you, is not here;
For I myself at this time have employ'd him.
And, sheriff, I will engage my word to thee,

102

That I will, by to-morrow dinner-time,
Send him to answer thee, or any man,
For any thing he shall be charged withal:
And so, let me entreat you leave the house.

I can promise you that that man is not here;
for at the moment he is in my employment.
And, Sheriff, I give you my word
that I will, by dinner time tomorrow,
send him to face you or any man
on any charges raised against him:
and so, I ask you to leave the house.

SHER.
I will, my lord. There are two gentlemen
Have in this robbery lost three hundred marks.

I will, my lord. There are two gentlemen
who have lost three hundred marks in this robbery

PRINCE.
It may be so:if he have robb'd these men,
He shall be answerable; and so, farewell.

That may be the case: if he has robbed these men,
he shall answer for it; and so, farewell.

SHER.
Good night, my noble lord.

Good night, my noble lord.

PRINCE.
I think it is good morrow, is it not?

I think it's good morning, isn't it?

SHER.
Indeed, my lord, I think't be two o'clock.

Indeed, my lord, I think it is two o'clock.

[Exit Sheriff and Carrier.]

PRINCE.
This oily rascal is known as well as Paul's. Go, call him forth.

This oily rascal is as well known as St Paul's Cathedral. Go, call him here.

POINTZ.
Falstaff!--fast asleep behind the arras, and snorting like a
horse.

*Falstaff! Fast asleep behind the arras, and snorting like a
horse.*

PRINCE.
Hark, how hard he fetches breath. Search his pockets.

[Pointz searches.]

What hast thou found?

Listen to how heavily he breathes. Search his pockets.

What have you found?

POINTZ.
Nothing but papers, my lord.

Just papers, my lord.

PRINCE.
Let's see what they be:read them.

Let's see what they are: read them.

POINTZ.
[reads]
Item, A capon, ...2s. 2d.
Item, Sauce, ... 4d.
Item, Sack two gallons ,. . . 5s. 8d.
Item, Anchovies and sack after supper,2s. 6d.
Item, Bread, ...ob.

Item, a chicken, two shillings and twopence.
Item, sauce, fourpence.
Item, sack, two gallons, five shillings and eightpence.

Item, anchovies and sack after supper, two shillings and sixpence.
Item, bread, halfpenny.

PRINCE.
O monstrous! but one half-pennyworth of bread to this intolerable
deal of sack! What there is else, keep close; we'll read it at more
advantage:there let him sleep till day.
I'll to the Court in the morning. We must all to the wars, and thy
place shall be honourable. I'll procure this fat rogue a charge of
foot; and I know his death will be a march of twelve-score. The money
shall be paid back again with advantage. Be with me betimes in the
morning; and so, good morrow, Pointz.

O monstrous! Just one halfpenny's worth of bread for this intolerable
quantity of sack! Hang onto whatever else there is; will read it when we have more time: let him
sleep there until daylight.
I'll go to the court in the morning. We must all go to the wars, and you shall have
an honourable position. I'll get this fat rogue command of a company
of infantry; I know he'll be dead within twelve paces. The money
shall be paid back with interest. Come to me early in the morning;
and so, good day, Pointz.

POINTZ.
Good morrow, good my lord.

Good day, my good lord.

[Exeunt.]

Act III

Scene I. Bangor. A Room in the Archdeacon's House.

[Enter Hotspur, Worcester, Mortimer, and Glendower.]

MORT.
These promises are fair, the parties sure,
And our induction full of prosperous hope.

These promises are fair, the parties are loyal,
and this opening shows every chance of success.

HOT.
Lord Mortimer,--and cousin Glendower,--Will you sit down?--
And uncle Worcester,--A plague upon it!I have forgot the map.

Lord Mortimer–and cousin Glendower–will you sit down?–
And uncle Worcester–dammit! I have forgotten the map.

GLEND.
No, here it is.
Sit, cousin Percy; sit, good cousin Hotspur;
For by that name as oft as Lancaster
Doth speak of you, his cheek looks pale, and with
A rising sigh he wisheth you in Heaven.

No, here it is.
Sit, cousin Percy; sit, good cousin Hotspur;
for it's by that name that Lancaster often
speaks of you, he turns pale, and with
a long sigh he wishes you were in heaven.

HOT.
And you in Hell, as oft as he hears Owen Glendower spoke of.

And you in hell, every time he hears Owen Glendower spoken of.

GLEND.
I cannot blame him:at my nativity
The front of heaven was full of fiery shapes,
Of burning cressets; ay, and at my birth

The frame and huge foundation of the Earth
Shaked like a coward.

I don't blame him: when I was born
the whole sky was full of fiery shapes,
like beacons; yes, and at my birth
the earth trembled from top to toe
like a coward.

HOT.
Why, so it would have done at the same season, if your mother's
cat had but kitten'd, though yourself had never been born.

Why, it would have done that at that time anyway, if it was
just your mother's cat having kittens, if you yourself had never been born.

GLEND.
I say the Earth did shake when I was born.

I'm telling you, the Earth shook when I was born.

HOT.
And I say the Earth was not of my mind, if you suppose as
fearing you it shook.

And I say that the Earth was thinking differently to me,
if you think it shook for fear of you.

GLEND.
The Heavens were all on fire, the Earth did tremble.

The heavens were all on fire, the Earth trembled.

HOT.
O, then th' Earth shook to see the Heavens on fire,
And not in fear of your nativity.
Diseased Nature oftentimes breaks forth
In strange eruptions; oft the teeming Earth
Is with a kind of colic pinch'd and vex'd
By the imprisoning of unruly wind
Within her womb; which, for enlargement striving,
Shakes the old beldam Earth, and topples down
Steeples and moss-grown towers. At your birth,

Our grandam Earth, having this distemperature,
In passion shook.

Oh, then the Earth shook to see the skies on fire,
and not out of fear at your birth.
Diseased nature often erupts
in peculiar ways, often the squirming earth
is pinched with a kind of stomach ache,
when some unruly wind gets trapped
deep down inside, and as it tries to swell
it shakes old grandmother Earth, and throws down
steeples and ancient towers. At your birth
our grandmother Earth had this illness,
and shook with passion.

GLEND.
Cousin, of many men
I do not bear these crossings. Give me leave
To tell you once again, that at my birth
The front of heaven was full of fiery shapes;
The goats ran from the mountains, and the herds
Were strangely clamorous to the frighted fields.
These signs have mark'd me extraordinary;
And all the courses of my life do show
I am not in the roll of common men.
Where is he living,--clipp'd in with the sea
That chides the banks of England, Scotland, Wales,--
Which calls me pupil, or hath read to me?
And bring him out that is but woman's son
Can trace me in the tedious ways of art,
And hold me pace in deep experiments.

Cousin, I wouldn't take these insults
from many men. Allow me
to tell you once again, that at my birth
the sky of heaven was full of fiery shapes;
the goats ran from the mountains, and the herds
shouted strange noises to the frightened fields.
These signs marked me out as extraordinary,
and everything I've done in my life shows
I am not like other men.
Show me anyone on this island bound by sea,
in England, Scotland or Wales,
who can call me his pupil or has tutored me?

Bring out anyone who is born of woman
who can follow me in the difficult paths of science,
who can keep up with me in complicated experiments.

HOT.
I think there is no man speaks better Welsh.--I'll to dinner.

I don't think any man speaks better Welsh. I'm going to dinner.

MORT.
Peace, cousin Percy; you will make him mad.

Quiet, cousin Percy; you will make him angry.

GLEND.
I can call spirits from the vasty deep.

I can call up spirits from the great ocean.

HOT.
Why, so can I, or so can any man;
But will they come when you do call for them?

Why, so can I, and so can any man;
but will they come when you call for them?

GLEND.
Why, I can teach you, cousin, to command the Devil.

Why, I can teach you, cousin, to summon up the Devil.

HOT.
And I can teach thee, coz, to shame the Devil
By telling truth:tell truth, and shame the Devil.
If thou have power to raise him, bring him hither,
And I'll be sworn I've power to shame him hence.
O, while you live, tell truth, and shame the Devil!

And I can teach you, cousin, to make the devil ashamed
by telling the truth: tell the truth, and shame the devil.
If you have the power to summon him, bring him here,
and I swear that I have the power to send him away again in shame.
Oh, while you live, tell the truth, and shame the devil!

MORT.

Come, come, no more of this unprofitable chat.

Come, come, no more of this useless talk.

GLEND.

Three times hath Henry Bolingbroke made head
Against my power; thrice from the banks of Wye
And sandy-bottom'd Severn have I sent
Him bootless home and weather-beaten back.

Henry Bolingbroke has launched attacks against me
three times; and three times I have sent him
home unsuccessful and weatherbeaten from the banks
of the Wye and the sandy bottomed Severn.

HOT.

Home without boots, and in foul weather too!
How 'scaped he agues, in the Devil's name!

Home without boots, and in foul weather too!
How the devil did he escape the fever?

GLEND.

Come, here's the map:shall we divide our right
According to our threefold order ta'en?

Come, here's the map; shall we divide
up to land according to the agreement we've made?

MORT.

Th' archdeacon hath divided it
Into three limits very equally.
England, from Trent and Severn hitherto,
By south and east is to my part assign'd:
All westward, Wales beyond the Severn shore,
And all the fertile land within that bound,
To Owen Glendower:--and, dear coz, to you
The remnant northward, lying off from Trent.
And our indentures tripartite are drawn;
Which being sealed interchangeably,--
A business that this night may execute,--
To-morrow, cousin Percy, you, and I,
And my good Lord of Worcester, will set forth

To meet your father and the Scottish power,
As is appointed us, at Shrewsbury.
My father Glendower is not ready yet,
Nor shall we need his help these fourteen days:--
[To Glend.] Within that space you may have drawn together
Your tenants, friends, and neighbouring gentlemen.

The Archdeacon has divided it
into thee very equal parts:
England, from the Trent and the Severn to here,
everything south and east of that is mine:
everything to the west, all of Wales beyond the shores of the Severn,
and all the fertile land inside those boundaries,
goes to Owen Glendower: and you, dear cousin,
take everything left north of the Trent.
Our contracts are signed in triplicate,
and once we have put our seals on them–
which is something we can do tonight–
tomorrow, cousin Percy, you and I,
and my good Lord of Worcester, will set out
to meet your father and the Scottish forces,
at Shrewsbury, as we have agreed.
My father Glendower is not ready yet,
and we won't need his help for a fortnight.
[to Glendower] within that time you may have gathered
your tenants, friends, and neighbouring gentlemen.

GLEND.
A shorter time shall send me to you, lords:
And in my conduct shall your ladies come;
From whom you now must steal, and take no leave,
For there will be a world of water shed
Upon the parting of your wives and you.

I'll be with you in a shorter time than that, lords:
and your ladies shall come under my escort;
from the moment you must sneak away from them without saying goodbye,
for there will be an ocean of water shed
when you part from your wives.

HOT.
Methinks my moiety, north from Burton here,
In quantity equals not one of yours.
See how this river comes me cranking in,

And cuts me from the best of all my land
A huge half-moon, a monstrous cantle out.
I'll have the current in this place damn'd up;
And here the smug and sliver Trent shall run
In a new channel, fair and evenly:
It shall not wind with such a deep indent,
To rob me of so rich a bottom here.

I don't think my share, north from Burton here,
at all matches your shares in size.
See how the river comes bending in on me,
and cuts me off from a great half moon
of all my best land, takes away a great portion.
I'll dam the river at this place,
and the smooth and silver Trent shall run
in a fair straight new channel:
it shan't cut such a deep course
that it can rob me of such a fine valley here.

GLEND.
Not wind? it shall, it must; you see it doth.

Not wind? It shall, it must; you can see that it does.

MORT.
Yea, but
Mark how he bears his, and runs me up
With like advantage on the other side;
Gelding th' opposed continent as much
As on the other side it takes from you.

Yes,
but look how the course of the river runs,
taking just as big a piece of my land
on the other side; we both get
an equal advantage.

WOR.
Yea, but a little charge will trench him here,
And on this north side win this cape of land;
And then he runneth straight and evenly.

Yes, but a little explosion could divert it here,
and on this north side he would win this piece of land;

and then it would run straight and even.

HOT.
I'll have it so:a little charge will do it.

I'll do it: a little explosion will do it.

GLEND.
I will not have it alter'd.

I won't have it altered.

HOT.
Will not you?

Won't you?

GLEND.
No, nor you shall not.

No, and neither will you.

HOT.
Who shall say me nay?

Who's going to say I can't?

GLEND.
Why, that will I.

Well, I will.

HOT.
Let me not understand you, then; speak it in Welsh.

Don't let me understand you then; say it in Welsh.

GLEND.
I can speak English, lord, as well as you;
For I was train'd up in the English Court;
Where, being but young, I framed to the harp
Many an English ditty lovely well,
And gave the tongue a helpful ornament,
A virtue that was never seen in you.

I can speak English, lord, as well as you;
for I was brought up in the English court;
where, as I was only young, I learnt to sing
many English songs beautifully well to the harp,
and added music to the words–
something you've never done.

HOT.
Marry, and I am glad of it with all my heart:
I had rather be a kitten, and cry mew,
Than one of these same metre ballet-mongers;
I had rather hear a brazen canstick turn'd,
Or a dry wheel grate on the axletree;
And that would set my teeth nothing on edge,
Nothing so much as mincing poetry:
'Tis like the forced gait of a shuffling nag.

Indeed, and I am extremely glad of it:
I would rather be a kitten, and meow,
than one of these rhythmic song writers;
I would rather hear a bronze candlestick on a lathe,
or a dry wheel grating on its axle;
that wouldn't set my teeth on edge half as much
as mincing poetry:
it's like the forced steps of a shuffling nag.

GLEND.
Come, you shall have Trent turn'd.

Come, you will change the course of the Trent.

HOT.
I do not care:I'll give thrice so much land
To any well-deserving friend;
But in the way of bargain, mark ye me,
I'll cavil on the ninth part of a hair.
Are the indentures drawn? shall we be gone?

I don't care: I will give three times as much land
to any well deserving friend;
but when it's a matter of an agreement, believe me,
I will argue to the last inch.
Are the contracts drawn up? Shall we go?

GLEND.
The Moon shines fair; you may away by night:
I'll in and haste the writer, and withal
Break with your wives of your departure hence:
I am afraid my daughter will run mad,
So much she doteth on her Mortimer.

The moon is shining fair; you can go by night:
I'll go and tell the writer to hurry, and also
break the news of your departure to your wives:
I'm afraid my daughter will go mad,
she adores her Mortimer so much.

[Exit.]

MORT.
Fie, cousin Percy! how you cross my father!

Dammit, cousin Percy! How you annoy my father!

HOT.
I cannot choose:sometimes he angers me
With telling me of the moldwarp and the ant,
Of the dreamer Merlin and his prophecies,
And of a dragon and a finless fish,
A clip-wing'd griffin and a moulten raven,
A couching lion and a ramping cat,
And such a deal of skimble-skamble stuff
As puts me from my faith. I tell you what,
He held me last night at the least nine hours
In reckoning up the several devils' names
That were his lacqueys:I cried hum, and well,
But mark'd him not a word. O, he's as tedious
As a tired horse, a railing wife;
Worse than a smoky house: I had rather live
With cheese and garlic in a windmill, far,
Than feed on cates and have him talk to me
In any summer-house in Christendom.

I can't help it: sometimes he annoys me
telling me about moles and ants,
of the dreamer Merlin and his prophecies,
and of a dragon and a fish without fins,

a wingless Griffin and a moulting raven,
a crouching lion and a leaping cat,
and such a lot of old claptrap
I find it hard to believe anything. I tell you what,
last night he kept me for at least nine hours
telling me the names of all the devils
who were his servants: I cried hum, and well well,
but he paid no attention. Oh, he's as boring
as a tired horse, a complaining wife;
worse than a smoky house: I would far rather live
with cheese and garlic in a windmill
than feed on delicacies and have him talking to me
in any summer house in Christendom.

MORT.
In faith, he is a worthy gentleman;
Exceedingly well-read, and profited
In strange concealments; valiant as a lion,
And wondrous affable, and as bountiful
As mines of India. Shall I tell you, cousin?
He holds your temper in a high respect,
And curbs himself even of his natural scope
When you do cross his humour; faith, he does:
I warrant you, that man is not alive
Might so have tempted him as you have done,
Without the taste of danger and reproof:
But do not use it oft, let me entreat you.

I swear, he is a good gentleman;
he's very well read, and expert
in secret arts; brave as a lion,
and amazingly friendly, and as bountiful
as the mines in India. Shall I tell you something, cousin?
He has a very great respect for you,
and reins in his natural inclinations
when you annoy him; I swear, he does:
I promise you, there isn't a man alive
who could have pushed him as far as you have done
without any danger or punishment:
but don't try too often, I beg you.

WOR.
In faith, my lord, you are too wilful-blame;
And since your coming hither have done enough

To put him quite beside his patience.
You must needs learn, lord, to amend this fault:
Though sometimes it show greatness, courage, blood--
And that's the dearest grace it renders you,--
Yet oftentimes it doth present harsh rage,
Defect of manners, want of government,
Pride, haughtiness, opinion, and disdain;
The least of which haunting a nobleman
Loseth men's hearts, and leaves behind a stain
Upon the beauty of all parts besides,
Beguiling them of commendation.

I swear, my lord, you are too wilful;
since he came here you've done enough
to put him quite out of temper.
You must learn, lord, not to do this:
although sometimes it can show greatness, courage, good breeding–
and it has given you that noble grace/
but often it looks like harsh anger,
a lack of manners, of self-control,
pride, haughtiness, arrogance and disdain;
and if a nobleman has any of these qualities
he will lose the hearts of men, and pollutes
all his good parts as well,
taking away people's good opinion of them.

HOT.
Well, I am school'd:good manners be your speed!
Here come our wives, and let us take our leave.

Well, I have been told: let's hope good manners win battles!
Here come our wives, let's say goodbye to them.

[Re-enter Glendower, with Lady Mortimer and Lady Percy.]

MORT.
This is the deadly spite that angers me,
My wife can speak no English, I no Welsh.

This is the terrible curse that angers me,
my wife cannot speak English, and I can't speak Welsh.

GLEND.
My daughter weeps:she will not part with you;

She'll be a soldier too, she'll to the wars.

My daughter weeps: she doesn't want to leave you;
she wants to be a soldier too, she wants to go to the war.

MORT.
Good father, tell her that she and my aunt Percy
Shall follow in your conduct speedily.

Good father, tell her that she and my aunt Percy
will soon follow under your escort.

[Glendower speaks to Lady Mortimer in Welsh, and she answers
him in the same.]

GLEND.
She's desperate here; a peevish self-will'd harlotry,
One that no persuasion can do good upon.

She is desperate here; she's being wilful and sullen,
there's nothing I can do to change her mind.

[Lady Mortimer speaks to Mortimer in Welsh.]

MORT.
I understand thy looks:that pretty Welsh
Which thou pour'st down from these swelling heavens
I am too perfect in; and, but for shame,
In such a parley should I answer thee.

[Lady Mortimer speaks to him again in Welsh.]

I understand thy kisses, and thou mine,
And that's a feeling disputation:
But I will never be a truant, love,
Till I have learn'd thy language; for thy tongue
Makes Welsh as sweet as ditties highly penn'd,
Sung by a fair queen in a Summer's bower,
With ravishing division, to her lute.

I understand your looks: the pretty Welsh
which is pouring down from those swelling heavens
is easy for me to read; and, if it wasn't for fear of being ashamed,
I would answer you in the same language.

I understand your kisses, and you understand mine,
and we can exchange our feelings:
but I will never leave off learning, love,
until I have learned your language; for your tongue
makes Welsh as sweet as the greatest poetry,
sung by a fair Queen in a summer glade,
playing brilliantly on her lute.

GLEND.
Nay, if you melt, then will she run mad.

No, if you start crying then she will go mad.

[Lady Mortimer speaks to Mortimer again in Welsh.]

MORT.
O, I am ignorance itself in this!

Oh, I don't understand a word of this!

GLEND.
She bids you on the wanton rushes lay you down,
And rest your gentle head upon her lap,
And she will sing the song that pleaseth you,
And on your eyelids crown the god of sleep,
Charming your blood with pleasing heaviness;
Making such difference betwixt wake and sleep,
As is the difference betwixt day and night,
The hour before the heavenly-harness'd team
Begins his golden progress in the East.

She asks you to lie down on the luxuriant rushes,
and rest your gentle head upon her lap,
and she will sing the song you like,
and send you off to sleep,
charming your blood with a sweet drowsiness,
making the same difference between waking and sleeping
as the difference between day and night,
the hour before the sun rises in the east.

MORT.
With all my heart I'll sit and hear her sing:
By that time will our book, I think, be drawn.

With all my heart I shall sit and hear her sing:
by that time I think our contract will be drawn up.

GLEND.
Do so:
An those musicians that shall play to you
Hang in the air a thousand leagues from hence,
And straight they shall be here:sit, and attend.

Do so:
and those musicians that will play to you
are in the air thousands of miles away,
and they will be here at once: sit, and listen.

HOT.
Come, Kate, thou art perfect in lying down:come, quick,
quick, that I may lay my head in thy lap.

Come, Kate, you're very good at lying down: come, quickly,
quickly, so I can put my head in your lap.

LADY P.
Go, ye giddy goose.

Give over, you giddy goose.

[The music plays.]

HOT.
Now I perceive the Devil understands Welsh;
And 'tis no marvel he's so humorous.
By'r Lady, he's a good musician.

Now I see the devil can speak Welsh;
it's no surprise he's so changeable.
I swear, he's a good musician.

LADY P.
Then should you be nothing but musical; for you are
altogether governed by humours. Lie still, ye thief, and hear
the lady sing in Welsh.

So you should be nothing but musical; for you are

*as changeable as anybody. Keep still, you scoundrel, and listen
to the lady singing in Welsh.*

HOT.
I had rather hear Lady, my brach, howl in Irish.

I would rather hear my bitch howl in Irish.

LADY P.
Wouldst thou have thy head broken?

Do you want a broken head?

HOT.
No.

No.

LADY P.
Then be still.

Then keep still.

HOT.
Neither; 'tis a woman's fault.

I shan't; that's for women.

LADY P.
Now God help thee!

Now God help you!

HOT.
Peace! she sings.

Hush! She's singing.

[A Welsh song by Lady Mortimer.]

Come, Kate, I'll have your song too.

Come, Kate, give us a song too.

LADY P.
Not mine, in good sooth.

I shan't, I swear.

HOT.
Not yours, in good sooth! 'Heart! you swear like a
comfit-maker's wife. Not mine, in good sooth; and, As true
as I live; and, As God shall mend me; and, As sure as day;
And givest such sarcenet surety for thy oaths,
As if thou ne'er walk'dst further than Finsbury.
Swear me, Kate, like a lady as thou art,
A good mouth-filling oath; and leave in sooth,
And such protest of pepper-gingerbread,
To velvet-guards and Sunday-citizens. Come, sing.

You shan't, you swear! By God! You swear like a
confectioner's wife. You shan't, you swear; and "as true
as I live" and "as God shall mend me" and "as sure as day";
your oaths are so insignificant one would think
you had never gone further than Finsbury.
Swear to me Kate, like the lady you are,
a good meaty oath; and leave saying "in truth"
and other such footling swearing
to the Sunday tourists. Come along, sing.

LADY P.
I will not sing.

I shall not sing.

HOT.
'Tis the next way to turn tailor, or be redbreast-teacher.
An the indentures be drawn, I'll away within these two hours;
and so, come in when ye will.

Alright, it only turns one into a tailor, or a songbird teacher.
Once the contracts are drawn up, I'll be off within two hours;
and so, come inside when you want.

[Exit.]

GLEND.
Come, come, Lord Mortimer; you are as slow

As hot Lord Percy is on fire to go.
By this our book's drawn; we'll but seal, and then
To horse immediately.

Come, come, Lord Mortimer; you are as reluctant
to go as hot Lord Percy is keen.
Our contract has been finished; we just have to seal it, and then
we'll go straight off.

MORT.
With all my heart.

I totally agree.

[Exeunt.]

Scene II. London. A Room in the Palace.

[Enter King Henry, Prince Henry, and Lords.]

KING.
Lords, give us leave; the Prince of Wales and I
Must have some private conference: but be near at hand,
For we shall presently have need of you.

[Exeunt Lords.]

I know not whether God will have it so,
For some displeasing service I have done,
That, in His secret doom, out of my blood
He'll breed revengement and a scourge for me;
But thou dost, in thy passages of life,
Make me believe that thou art only mark'd
For the hot vengeance and the rod of Heaven
To punish my mistreadings. Tell me else,
Could such inordinate and low desires,
Such poor, such base, such lewd, such mean attempts,
Such barren pleasures, rude society,
As thou art match'd withal and grafted to,
Accompany the greatness of thy blood,
And hold their level with thy princely heart?

Lords, excuse us; the Prince of Wales and I
must have a private talk: but stay close by,
for I shallneed you soon.

I don't know whether God has arranged it like this,
thanks to something I have done wrong,
and that he has passed sentence that my own flesh and blood
should be the instrument of revenge and a whip for me;
but the way you live your life
makes me believe that you have been chosen
as the instrument of revenge and the rod of heaven,
to punish my errors. Tell me otherwise
how such unworthy and low desires,
such wretched base exploits,

such empty pleasures andvulgar society
such as you associate with can
be matched with the greatness of your blood,
and find a place within your princely heart.

PRINCE.
So please your Majesty, I would I could
Quit all offences with as clear excuse
As well as I am doubtless I can purge
Myself of many I am charged withal:
Yet such extenuation let me beg,
As, in reproof of many tales devised
By smiling pick-thanks and base news-mongers,--
Which oft the ear of greatness needs must hear,--
I may, for some things true, wherein my youth
Hath faulty wander'd and irregular,
Find pardon on my true submission.

If you please, your Majesty, I wish I could
acquit myself of all offences with as good an excuse
as I am sure that I can supply for
many of the ones I'm charged with:
but let me ask for this forgiveness,
perhaps when I prove that many of the tales
were invented by malicious and low gossips–
they are always present around royalty–
I might be forgiven for some of the things
I have done wrong due to my wayward youth
by making a clean breast of everything.

KING.
God pardon thee! Yet let me wonder, Harry,
At thy affections, which do hold a wing
Quite from the flight of all thy ancestors.
Thy place in Council thou hast rudely lost,
Which by thy younger brother is supplied;
And art almost an alien to the hearts
Of all the Court and princes of my blood:
The hope and expectation of thy time
Is ruin'd; and the soul of every man
Prophetically does forethink thy fall.
Had I so lavish of my presence been,
So common-hackney'd in the eyes of men,
So stale and cheap to vulgar company,

Opinion, that did help me to the crown,
Had still kept loyal to possession,
And left me in reputeless banishment,
A fellow of no mark nor likelihood.
By being seldom seen, I could not stir
But, like a comet, I was wonder'd at;
That men would tell their children, This is he;
Others would say, Where, which is Bolingbroke?
And then I stole all courtesy from Heaven,
And dress'd myself in such humility,
That I did pluck allegiance from men's hearts,
Loud shouts and salutations from their mouths,
Even in the presence of the crowned King.
Thus did I keep my person fresh and new;
My presence, like a robe pontifical,
Ne'er seen but wonder'd at:and so my state,
Seldom but sumptuous, showed like a feast,
And won by rareness such solemnity.
The skipping King, he ambled up and down
With shallow jesters and rash bavin wits,
Soon kindled and soon burnt; carded his state,
Mingled his royalty, with capering fools;
Had his great name profaned with their scorns;
And gave his countenance, against his name,
To laugh at gibing boys, and stand the push
Of every beardless vain comparative;
Grew a companion to the common streets,
Enfeoff'd himself to popularity;
That, being dally swallow'd by men's eyes,
They surfeited with honey, and began
To loathe the taste of sweetness, whereof a little
More than a little is by much too much.
So, when he had occasion to be seen,
He was but as the cuckoo is in June,
Heard, not regarded; seen, but with such eyes
As, sick and blunted with community,
Afford no extraordinary gaze,
Such as is bent on sun-like majesty
When it shines seldom in admiring eyes;
But rather drowsed, and hung their eyelids down,
Slept in his face, and render'd such aspect
As cloudy men use to their adversaries,
Being with his presence glutted, gorged, and full.
And in that very line, Harry, stand'st thou;

For thou hast lost thy princely privilege
With vile participation:not an eye
But is a-weary of thy common sight,
Save mine, which hath desired to see thee more;
Which now doth that I would not have it do,
Make blind itself with foolish tenderness.

May God pardon you! But I must say I'm astonished, Harry,
at the things you like, which are quite different to those
preferred by all your ancestors.
Through rudeness you lost your place in the Council,
which is filled by your younger brother,
and you are completely alienated from the hearts
of the whole court and your own brothers:
the hopes and expectations we had of you
have vanished, and every man secretly thinks
he can predict your downfall.
If I had appeared so much in public,
been such a workaday person in men's eyes,
the public, who helped me gain the Crown,
would have stayed loyal to Richard,
and left me to live as an unknown exile,
a fellow of no fame or promise.
By only being seen seldom, I couldn't move
without being wondered at like a comet,
so men would tell their children, "This is him!"
Others would say, "Where, which one is Bolingbroke?"
Then I assumed a courtly demeanour from heaven,
and make myself look so humble
that I took loyalty from men's hearts,
loud shouts and praise from their mouths,
even in the presence of the crowned King.
So I kept myself fresh and new,
for me to appear was like an archbishop's robe,
always marvelled at when seen, and so my royalty,
not seen often but always magnificent when it was,
was like a feast, and won respect through being rare.
The frivolous king, he wandered up and down,
with shallow gestures, superficial wits,
quick with a joke but quickly out of jokes, he degraded his dignity,
mixed his royalty with capering fools,
had his great name disgraced with their scorn,
and ruined his authority by laughing at the jokes
of foolish boys, and tolerating the impudence

of every vain young insulter,
he became well known in the common streets,
surrendering himself to popularity,
so that, being seen daily by everybody,
they had too much of him, like honey, they began
to hate the taste of sweetness, of which a little
more than a little is far too much.
So, when he wanted to appear as King,
he was like the cuckoo in June,
heard, but not noted; seen, but with eyes that,
made stale through constant association,
gave him no wondering gaze,
like the ones given to sunlike Majesty
when it only shines rarely an admiring eyes,
instead they were drowsy and close their eyes,
slept in front of him, and behaved towards him
as argumentative men behave to their enemies,
having already had far too much of seeing him.
And that is exactly the way you are, Harry,
you have lost your princely dignity
by joining in with the lowest. Everybody
is sick of seeing you all the time,
apart from me, who wanted to see you more,
and now I'm doing what I don't want to do,
clouding my eyes with the tears of foolish tenderness.

PRINCE.
I shall hereafter, my thrice-gracious lord,
Be more myself.

From now on, my triply–gracious lord,
I shall remember my position.

KING.
For all the world,
As thou art to this hour, was Richard then
When I from France set foot at Ravenspurg;
And even as I was then is Percy now.
Now, by my sceptre, and my soul to boot,
He hath more worthy interest to the state
Than thou, the shadow of succession;
For, of no right, nor colour like to right,
He doth fill fields with harness in the realm,
Turns head against the lion's armed jaws;

And, being no more in debt to years than thou,
Leads ancient lords and reverend bishops on
To bloody battles and to bruising arms.
What never-dying honour hath he got
Against renowned Douglas! whose high deeds,
Whose hot incursions, and great name in arms,
Holds from all soldiers chief majority
And military title capital
Through all the kingdoms that acknowledge Christ:
Thrice hath this Hotspur, Mars in swathing-clothes,
This infant warrior, in his enterprises
Discomfited great Douglas; ta'en him once,
Enlarged him, and made a friend of him,
To fill the mouth of deep defiance up,
And shake the peace and safety of our throne.
And what say you to this? Percy, Northumberland,
Th' Archbishop's Grace of York, Douglas, and Mortimer
Capitulate against us, and are up.
But wherefore do I tell these news to thee?
Why, Harry, do I tell thee of my foes,
Which art my near'st and dearest enemy?
Thou that art like enough,--through vassal fear,
Base inclination, and the start of spleen,--
To fight against me under Percy's pay,
To dog his heels, and curtsy at his frowns,
To show how much thou art degenerate.

You are exactly the same
at the moment as Richard was when
I landed at Ravenspurgh from France,
and Percy is like I was then.
Now I swear by my sceptre, and my soul as well,
he has qualities which suit him for a claim to the state,
while you just have the weak one of heredity.
Without any right, or anything resembling a right,
he fills the fields of the kingdom with armed men,
turning his head towards the Royal Army,
and though he is no older than you
he leads ancient lords and distinguished bishops
into bloody battles, and bruising fights.
What immortal honour he gained
against the famous Douglas! Douglas, whose
great deeds, whose hearty invasions and great
reputation as a soldier make him acknowledged by

all other soldiers as the greatest of them
throughout all the kingdoms of Christendom.
Three times this Hotspur, Mars in swaddling clothes,
this child warrior, has in his efforts
unsettled great Douglas, captured him once,
honoured him, and made a friend of him,
to increase the chorus of defiance,
and shake the peace and safety of my throne.
And what you think of this? Percy, Northumberland,
the Archbishop of York, Douglas, Mortimer,
have all signed an agreement against me and are revolting.
But why do I tell you this news?
Why, Harry, do I tell you of my enemies,
when you are my nearest and dearest enemy?
You who are likely enough, through peasant fear,
low inclination, and a fit of ill temper,
to fight against me in Percy's service,
to follow at his heels, and curtsy at his frowns,
to show what a degenerate you are.

PRINCE.
Do not think so; you shall not find it so:
And God forgive them that so much have sway'd
Your Majesty's good thoughts away from me!
I will redeem all this on Percy's head,
And, in the closing of some glorious day,
Be bold to tell you that I am your son;
When I will wear a garment all of blood,
And stain my favour in a bloody mask,
Which, wash'd away, shall scour my shame with it:
And that shall be the day, whene'er it lights,
That this same child of honour and renown,
This gallant Hotspur, this all-praised knight,
And your unthought-of Harry, chance to meet.
For every honour sitting on his helm,
Would they were multitudes, and on my head
My shames redoubled! for the time will come,
That I shall make this northern youth exchange
His glorious deeds for my indignities.
Percy is but my factor, good my lord,
T' engross up glorious deeds on my behalf;
And I will call hall to so strict account,
That he shall render every glory up,
Yea, even the slightest worship of his time,

Or I will tear the reckoning from his heart.
This, in the name of God, I promise here:
The which if I perform, and do survive,
I do beseech your Majesty, may salve
The long-grown wounds of my intemperance:
If not, the end of life cancels all bands;
And I will die a hundred thousand deaths
Ere break the smallest parcel of this vow.

Do not think so, this will not happen;
and God forgive those who have persuaded
your Majesty to think of me like this!
I will redeem myself by fighting Percy,
and at the end of some glorious battle
I shall boldly tell you I am your son,
when my garments will be covered in blood,
and my face covered with a bloody mask,
which, when I wash it away, will wash my shame away with it;
and that will be the day, whenever it comes,
that this renowned and honoured man,
this gallant Hotspur, this widely praised knight,
and your disregarded Harry shall meet.
For every honour that he has won,
I wish each one was multiplied, and that
all my shame could be doubled! For the time will come
when I shall make this young Northerner exchange
his glorious deeds for my shames.
Percy is just my agent, my good lord,
who gathers up glorious deeds on my behalf,
and I will call him to such a strict account
that he will give up every glory he has won,
every ounce of honour in his life,
or I will tear the payment out of his heart.
I promise this now in the name of God,
and if He is good enough to let me succeed,
I beg your Majesty to let that heal
the pain I have caused him through my bad behaviour:
if not, death cancels all debts,
and I will die a hundred thousand deaths
before I break the tiniest part of this promise.

KING.
A hundred thousand rebels die in this.
Thou shalt have charge and sovereign trust herein.--

[Enter Sir Walter Blunt.]

How now, good Blunt! thy looks are full of speed.

A hundred thousand rebels die as you speak.
You shall have the command and the trust of your king.
Hello there, good Blunt! You look in a hurry.

BLUNT.
So is the business that I come to speak of.
Lord Mortimer of Scotland hath sent word
That Douglas and the English rebels met
Th' eleventh of this month at Shrewsbury:
A mighty and a fearful head they are,
If promises be kept on every hand,
As ever offer'd foul play in a State.

What I've come to tell you demands hurry.
Lord Mortimer of Scotland has sent word
that Douglas and the English rebels met
on the eleventh of this month at Shrewsbury:
they are as great and as fearful a force,
if everyone keeps their promises,
as has ever tried to overthrow a state.

KING.
The Earl of Westmoreland set forth to-day;
With him my son, Lord John of Lancaster;
For this advertisement is five days old.
On Wednesday next you, Harry, shall set forward;
On Thursday we ourselves will march:
Our meeting is Bridgenorth:and, Harry, you
Shall march through Glostershire; by which account,
Our business valued, some twelve days hence
Our general forces at Bridgenorth shall meet.
Our hands are full of business:let's away;
Advantage feeds him fat, while men delay.

[Exeunt.]

The Earl of Westmorland set out today;
with him went my son, Lord John of Lancaster;
for this information is five days old.

Next Wednesday you, Harry, shall set out;
on Thursday I will march myself:
we shall rendezvous at Bridgnorth: and, Harry, you
shall march through Gloucestershire; by my reckoning,
for everything we have to do, we shall meet twelve days from now
with our whole army at Bridgnorth.
We have plenty to do: let's get going;
the enemy will gain an advantage if we delay.

Scene III. Eastcheap. A Room in the Boar's-Head Tavern.

[Enter Falstaff and Bardolph.]

FAL.
Bardolph, am I not fallen away vilely since this last action? do I
not bate? do I not dwindle? Why, my skin hangs about me like an
old lady's loose gown; I am withered like an old apple-John.
Well, I'll repent, and that suddenly, while I am in some liking; I
shall be out of heart shortly, and then I shall have no strength to
repent.
An I have not forgotten what the inside of a church is made of, I
am a peppercorn, a brewer's horse:the inside of a church!
Company, villainous company, hath been the spoil of me.

*Bardolph, haven't I declined terribly since this last exploit? Haven't I
lost weight? Aren't I shrinking? Why, my skin hangs on me like an
old lady's dressing gown; I am withered like an old apple.
Well, I'll repent, and do it suddenly, while I'm still whole; I
shall be in such poor condition soon that I shall have no strength to repent.
If I can remember what the inside of a church looks like, I
am a peppercorn, a brewer's horse: the inside of a church!
Company, evil company, has been the death of me.*

BARD.
Sir John, you are so fretful, you cannot live long.

Sir John, you worry so much, you can't live long.

FAL.
Why, there is it:come, sing me a song; make me merry. I was as
virtuously given as a gentleman need to be; virtuous enough; swore
little; diced not above seven times a week; paid money that I borrowed
--three or four times; lived well, and in good compass:and now I live
out of all order, out of all compass.

*Why, that's it: come on, sing their songs; make me merry. I was as
good as a gentleman needs to be; good enough; I didn't swear
much; didn't gamble more than seven times a week; paid money that I had borrowed
—three or four times; lived well, within good limits: and now I live*

all disordered, with no limits.

BARD.
Why, you are so fat, Sir John, that you must needs be out of all
compass, --out of all reasonable compass, Sir John.

*Why, you are so fat, Sir John, that you will always be
beyond the limit–beyond any reasonable limit, Sir John.*

FAL.
Do thou amend thy face, and I'll amend my life:thou art our admiral,
thou bearest the lantern in the poop,--but 'tis in the nose of thee;
thou art the Knight of the Burning Lamp.

*You change your face, and I'll change my lifestyle: you are our Admiral,
you carry the lantern for our ship–that's your glowing red nose,
you are the Knight of the Burning Lamp.*

BARD.
Why, Sir John, my face does you no harm.

Why, Sir John, my face does you no harm.

FAL.
No, I'll be sworn; I make as good use of it as many a man doth of a
death's-head or a memento mori:I never see thy face but I think upon
hell-fire, and Dives that lived in purple; for there he is in his robes,
burning, burning. If thou wert any way given to virtue, I would swear
by thy face; my oath should be, By this fire, that's God's angel:but
thou art altogether given over; and wert indeed, but for the light in
thy face, the son of utter darkness. When thou rann'st up Gad's-hill in
the night to catch my horse, if I did not think thou hadst been an ignis
fatuus or a ball of wildfire, there's no purchase in money. O, thou art
a perpetual triumph, an everlasting bonfire-light! Thou hast saved me a
thousand marks in links and torches, walking with thee in the night
betwixt tavern and tavern:but the sack that thou hast drunk me would
have bought me lights as good cheap at the dearest chandler's in Europe.
I have maintain'd that salamander of yours with fire any time this
two-and-thirty years; God reward me for it!

*No, I swear; I make good use of it as many men do of
death's heads or Memento Mori: I never see your face without thinking of
hellfire, and Dives who lived in purple; for there he is in his robes,
burning, burning. If there was any virtue in you, I would swear*

136

by your face; my oath would be, "By this fire, that's God's angel!": but
you have gone over completely to the other side, and apart from the light in your face,
you are the son of utter darkness. When you ran up Gadshill in
the night to catch my horse, if I didn't think you were an explosion or ball
lightning then money can't buy anything. Oh, you are
a permanent beacon, and everlasting bonfire! You have saved me a
thousand marks in flares and torches, walking with you at night
between taverns: but the sack that I have bought you would
have paid for lights at half the price from the most expensive shop in Europe.
I have provided fuel for that likes of yours for the past
thirty-two years; may God reward me for it!

BARD.
'Sblood, I would my face were in your stomach!

By God, I could wish it was burning up your stomach!

FAL.
God-a-mercy! so should I be sure to be heart-burn'd.--

[Enter the Hostess.]

How now, Dame Partlet the hen! have you enquir'd yet who
pick'd my pocket?

Lord have mercy! Then I would definitely have heartburn—

hello there, my old chicken! Have you found out yet who
picked my pocket?

HOST.
Why, Sir John, what do you think, Sir John? do you think I
keep thieves in my house? I have search'd, I have inquired,
so has my husband, man by man, boy by boy, servant by servant:
the tithe of a hair was never lost in my house before.

Why, Sir John, what do you think, St John? Do you think I'd
allow thieves in my house? I have looked, I have question,
so has my husband, every man, every boy, every servant:
no one ever lost the tenth of a hair before in my house.

FAL.
Ye lie, hostess:Bardolph was shaved, and lost many a hair; and
I'll be sworn my pocket was pick'd. Go to, you are a woman, go.

You're lying, landlady: Bardolph was shaved, and lost many hairs; and
I'll swear my pocket was picked. Get away, you are a woman, get away.

HOST.
Who, I? no; I defy thee:God's light, I was never call'd so in
mine own house before.

Who, me? No; I defy you; by God, I was never called that in
my own house before.

FAL.
Go to, I know you well enough.

Get away, I know you well enough.

HOST.
No, Sir John; you do not know me, Sir John. I know you, Sir John:
you owe me money, Sir John; and now you pick a quarrel to beguile me
of it: I bought you a dozen of shirts to your back.

No, Sir John; you do not know me, Sir John. I know you, Sir John:
you owe me money, Sir John; and now you start a quarrel to take
my mind off it: I bought you a dozen shirts to wear.

FAL.
Dowlas, filthy dowlas:I have given them away to bakers' wives,
and they have made bolters of them.

The worst sort of rough cloth: I have given them away to bakers' wives,
and they have made them into pudding cloths.

HOST.
Now, as I am a true woman, holland of eight shillings an ell.
You owe money here besides, Sir John, for your diet and by-drinkings,
and money lent you, four-and-twenty pound.

Now, as I am an honest woman, they were made of fine lawn at eight shillings a yard.
You owe money here as well, Sir John, for your food and your drinks between meals,
and for money lent to you, twenty-four pounds.

FAL.
He had his part of it; let him pay.

He had some of it; let him pay.

HOST.
He? alas, he is poor; he hath nothing.

Him? Alas, he is poor; he has nothing.

FAL.
How! poor? look upon his face; what call you rich? let
them coin his nose, let them coin his cheeks:I'll not pay a
denier. What, will you make a younker of me? shall I not take
mine ease in mine inn, but I shall have my pocket pick'd? I have
lost a seal-ring of my grandfather's worth forty mark.

*What! Poor? Look on his face; what do you call rich? Let them
stamp his nose, let them stamp his cheeks: I won't pay
a farthing. What, do you think I'm wet behind the ears? Can I not
relax in my own inn without having my pocket picked? I have
lost a signet ring of my grandfather's which was worth forty marks.*

HOST.
O Jesu, I have heard the Prince tell him, I know not how oft,
that that ring was copper!

*O Jesus, I don't know how often I've heard the Prince tell him
that that ring was made of copper!*

FAL.
How! the Prince is a Jack, a sneak-cup:'sblood, an he were
here, I would cudgel him like a dog, if he would say so.--

[Enter Prince Henry and Pointz, marching.Falstaff meets them,
playing on his truncheon like a fife.]

How now, lad? is the wind in that door, i'faith? must we all
march?

*What! The Prince is a knave, a sneaking rascal: by God, if he were
here, I would beat him like a dog, if he said that–*

*What's up, lad? Is that the way the wind blows, by God? Must we all
march?*

BARD.

Yea, two-and-two, Newgate-fashion.

Yes, two by two, prison style.

HOST.
My lord, I pray you, hear me.

My Lord, I beg you, listen to me.

PRINCE.
What say'st thou, Mistress Quickly? How doth thy husband? I love him well; he is an honest man.

What is it, Mistress Quickly? How is your husband? I like him very much; he is an honest man.

HOST.
Good my lord, hear me.

My good lord, listen to me.

FAL.
Pr'ythee, let her alone, and list to me.

Please, ignore her, and listen to me.

PRINCE.
What say'st thou, Jack?

What are you saying, Jack?

FAL.
The other night I fell asleep here behind the arras, and had my pocket pick'd:this house is turn'd bawdy-house; they pick pockets.

The other night I fell asleep here behind the curtain, and had my pocket picked: this house has become a brothel; they pick pockets.

PRINCE.
What didst thou lose, Jack?

What did you lose, Jack?

FAL.

Wilt thou believe me, Hal? three or four bonds of forty pound
a-piece and a seal-ring of my grandfather's.

*Will you believe me, Hal? Three or four bonds of forty pounds
each, and a signet ring of my grandfather's.*

PRINCE.
A trifle, some eight-penny matter.

A trifle, worth about eightpence.

HOST.
So I told him, my lord; and I said I heard your Grace say so;
and, my lord, he speaks most vilely of you, like a foul-mouth'd
man as he is; and said he would cudgel you.

*That's what I said to him, my lord; and I said I had heard your Grace say so;
and, my lord, he spoke horribly about you, like the foulmouthed
man he is; and he said he would beat you.*

PRINCE.
What! he did not?

What! He didn't?

HOST.
There's neither faith, truth, nor womanhood in me else.

If I'm lying I have no faith, honesty or womanhood in me.

FAL.
There's no more faith in thee than in a stew'd prune; nor no more
truth in thee than in a drawn fox; and, for woman-hood, Maid Marian
may be the deputy's wife of the ward to thee. Go, you thing, go.

*There is no more faith in you than in a common tart; no more
truth in you than in a hunted fox; and as for womanhood, maid Marian
would be a model of respectability compared to you. Go away, you object.*

HOST.
Say, what thing? what thing?I am an honest man's wife:and,
setting thy knighthood aside, thou art a knave to call me so.

Object? Object? I am the wife of an honest man: and,

forgetting your knighthood, you are a knave to call me that.

FAL.
Setting thy womanhood aside, thou art a beast to say otherwise.

Forgetting your womanhood, you are a beast to say different.

HOST.
Say, what beast, thou knave, thou?

You're calling me a beast, you knave, what sort of beast?

FAL.
What beast!why, an otter.

What sort? Why, an otter.

PRINCE.
An otter, Sir John, why an otter?

An otter, Sir John, why an otter?

FAL.
Why, she's neither fish nor flesh; a man knows not where to have
her.

Why, she is neither fish nor meat; a man doesn't know how to take her.

HOST.
Thou art an unjust man in saying so; thou or any man knows where
to have me, thou knave, thou!

*You are a dishonest man to say so; you or any man knows how
to take me, you knave, you!*

PRINCE.
Thou say'st true, hostess; and he slanders thee most grossly.

You're telling the truth, landlady; and he is insulting you terribly.

HOST.
So he doth you, my lord; and said this other day you ought him a
thousand pound.

He does the same to you, my lord; he said the other day you owed him a thousand pounds.

PRINCE.
Sirrah, do I owe you a thousand pound?

Sir, do I owe you a thousand pounds?

FAL.

A thousand pound, Hal! a million:thy love is worth a million; thou owest me thy love.

A thousand pounds, Hal!A million: your love is worth a million; you owe me your love.

HOST.
Nay, my lord, he call'd you Jack, and said he would cudgel you.

No, my lord, he called you a knave, and said he would beat you.

FAL.
Did I, Bardolph?

Did I, Bardolph?

BARD.
Indeed, Sir John, you said so.

Indeed, Sir John, that's what you said.

FAL.
Yea, if he said my ring was copper.

Yes, if he said my ring was copper.

PRINCE.
I say 'tis copper:darest thou be as good as thy word now?

I say it is copper: are you going to keep your word now?

FAL.
Why, Hal, thou know'st, as thou art but man, I dare; but as thou art prince, I fear thee as I fear the roaring of the lion's whelp.

*Why, Hal, you know, I would dare to fight you as a man; but as you
are Prince, I fear you as I fear the roaring of a lion cub.*

PRINCE.
And why not as the lion?

And why not the roaring of a lion?

FAL.
The King himself is to be feared as the lion:dost thou think I'll
fear thee as I fear thy father? nay, an I do, I pray God my girdle
break.

*The King himself is to be frightened of as a lion: do you think I'll
be as afraid of you as I am of your father? If I am, I pray to God
for my belt to break.*

PRINCE.
Sirrah, there's no room for faith, truth, nor honesty in this
bosom of thine; it is all fill'd up with midriff.
Charge an honest woman with picking thy pocket! why, thou whoreson,
impudent, emboss'd rascal, if there were anything in thy pocket but
tavern-reckonings, and one poor pennyworth of sugar-candy to make thee
long-winded,--if thy pocket were enrich'd with any other injuries but
these, I am a villain:and yet you will stand to it; you will not
pocket-up wrong. Art thou not ashamed!

*Sir, there is no room for faith, truth or honesty in this
heart of yours; it's all filled up with stomach.
Charge an honest woman with picking your pocket! Why, you son of a bitch,
impudent fake rascal, if there was anything in your pocket apart from
tavern bills, and a poor pennyworth of sugar candy to give you
energy–if your pockets had anything apart from these things
in them, I am a villain: and yet you stick by it; you
won't admit to your lies! Aren't you ashamed?*

FAL.
Dost thou hear, Hal? thou know'st, in the state of innocency Adam fell;
and what should poor Jack Falstaff do in the days of villainy?
Thou see'st I have more flesh than another man; and therefore more
frailty. You confess, then, you pick'd my pocket?

What do you think, Hal? You know that Adam fell in a state of innocence;

so how should poor JackFalstaff manage in these evil days?
You see I have more flesh than other men; and therefore more
weaknesses. You admit, then, that you picked my pocket?

PRINCE.
It appears so by the story.

That's what it looks like.

FAL.
Hostess, I forgive thee:go, make ready breakfast; love thy husband,
look to thy servants, cherish thy guests:thou shalt find me tractable
to any honest reason; thou see'st I am pacified.--Still?Nay, pr'ythee,
be gone.

[Exit Hostess.]

Now, Hal, to the news at Court:for the robbery, lad, how is
that answered?

Hostess, I forgive you: go and get breakfast ready; love your husband,
watch your servants, value your guests: you shall find me amenable
to any sort of honesty; you see I am pacified–still here? No, please,
be gone.

Now, Hal, give us news of the court: what reaction is there, lad,
to that robbery?

PRINCE.
O, my sweet beef, I must still be good angel to thee:the money
is paid back again.

Oh, my sweet ox, I must still be your good angel: the money
has been repaid.

FAL.
O, I do not like that paying back; 'tis a double labour.

Oh, I don't like repayments; it's twice the work.

PRINCE.
I am good friends with my father, and may do any thing.

I am good friends with my father, and can do anything.

FAL.

Rob me the exchequer the first thing thou doest, and do it with
unwash'd hands too.

*Rob the Treasury for me as the first thing you do, and don't
stand on ceremony.*

BARD.

Do, my lord.

Do, my lord.

PRINCE.

I have procured thee, Jack, a charge of Foot.

I have obtained for you, Jack, command of some infantry.

FAL.

I would it had been of Horse. Where shall I find one that can steal
well? O, for a fine thief, of the age of two-and-twenty or thereabouts!
I am heinously unprovided. Well, God be thanked for these rebels; they
offend none but the virtuous:I laud them, I praise them.

I would rather it had been cavalry. Where can I find a good thief?
Oh, for a fine thief, aged about twenty-two or so!
I am horribly unprepared. Well, thank God for these rebels, very
only offend the virtuous: I praise them.

PRINCE.
Bardolph,--

Bardolph–

BARD.
My lord?

My lord?

PRINCE.
Go bear this letter to Lord John of Lancaster,

My brother John; this to my Lord of Westmoreland.--

146

[Exit Bardolph.]

Go, Pointz, to horse, to horse; for thou and I
Have thirty miles to ride yet ere dinner-time.--

[Exit Pointz.]

Meet me to-morrow, Jack, i' the Temple-hall
At two o'clock in th' afternoon:
There shalt thou know thy charge; and there receive
Money and order for their furniture.
The land is burning; Percy stands on high;
And either they or we must lower lie.

Take this letter to Lord John of Lancaster,
to my brother John, and this one to my Lord of Westmorland.

Go, Peto, get the horses, for you and I
still have thirty miles to ride before dinner time.

Jack, meet me tomorrow in the Temple Hall
at two o'clock in the afternoon:
you shall meet your command, and receive
money to buy their equipment.
The land is burning, Percy is winning,
and either we or they must go to their graves.

[Exit.]

FAL.
Rare words! brave world!--Hostess, my breakfast; come:--
O, I could wish this tavern were my drum!

Great words! Brave world! Hostess, bring my breakfast—
O, I wish this tavern was my headquarters!

[Exit.]

Act IV

Scene I. The Rebel Camp near Shrewsbury.

[Enter Hotspur, Worcester, and Douglas.]

HOT.
Well said, my noble Scot:if speaking truth
In this fine age were not thought flattery,
Such attribution should the Douglas have,
As not a soldier of this season's stamp
Should go so general-current through the world.
By God, I cannot flatter; I defy
The tongues of soothers; but a braver place
In my heart's love hath no man than yourself:
Nay, task me to my word; approve me, lord.

Well said, noble Scotsman: if telling the truth
wasn't thought of as flattery in this fine age,
Douglas should be thought of as
the most perfect example of a soldier
living in this age of the world.
By God, I am no flatterer; I hate
smooth talkers; but there's not a man
who has such a good place in my heart as you.
Go on, my lord, you can ask me to prove it.

DOUG.
Thou art the king of honour:
No man so potent breathes upon the ground
But I will beard him.

You are the king of honour;
there's no man so powerful
that I won't beat him.

HOT.
Do so, and 'tis well.--

[Enter a Messenger with letters.]

What letters hast thou there?--I can but thank you.

Do that, and all will be well.

What are those letters you have there? I can only thank you.

MESS.
These letters come from your father.

These letters come from your father.

HOT.
Letters from him! why comes he not himself?

Letters from him! Why hasn't he come himself?

MESS.
He cannot come, my lord; he's grievous sick.

He can't come, my lord; he's very ill.

HOT.
Zwounds! how has he the leisure to be sick
In such a justling time? Who leads his power?
Under whose government come they along?

*By God! Where does he find the time to be ill
in such fast moving times? Who's leading his forces?
Who is directing them as they come?*

MESS.
His letters bears his mind, not I, my lord.

His letters say what he thinks, my lord, not me.

WOR.
I pr'ythee, tell me, doth he keep his bed?

Please tell me, is he bedridden?

MESS.
He did, my lord, four days ere I set forth,
And at the time of my departure thence
He was much fear'd by his physicians.

He was, my lord, for four days before I set out,
and when I left there
his doctors feared for his life.

WOR.
I would the state of time had first been whole
Ere he by sickness had been visited:
His health was never better worth than now.

I wish these matters has come to fruition
before he became ill:
he would have been very valuable to us.

HOT.
Sick now! droop now! this sickness doth infect
The very life-blood of our enterprise;
'Tis catching hither, even to our camp.
He writes me here, that inward sickness,--
And that his friends by deputation could not
So soon be drawn; no did he think it meet
To lay so dangerous and dear a trust
On any soul removed, but on his own.
Yet doth he give us bold advertisement,
That with our small conjunction we should on,
To see how fortune is disposed to us;
For, as he writes, there is no quailing now,
Because the King is certainly possess'd
Of all our purposes. What say you to it?

Ill now!Flagging now!This sickness infects
the very heart of our plans;
it will affect us even here in our camp.
He writes to me of his illness –
and that he couldn't get any friends to stand in
for him at such short notice; nor did he think
it fitting to lay such a dangerous and important task
on anyone but himself.
but he gives us very strong advice
to proceed with our plans,
to see what fortune might bring;
for, as he writes, there is no going back now,
because the King certainly has information
about our intentions.What do you say?

WOR.
Your father's sickness is a maim to us.

Your father's sickness is a setback.

HOT.
A perilous gash, a very limb lopp'd off:--
And yet, in faith, 'tis not; his present want
Seems more than we shall find it. Were it good
To set the exact wealth of all our states
All at one cast? to set so rich a main
On the nice hazard of one doubtful hour?
It were not good; for therein should we read
The very bottom and the soul of hope,
The very list, the very utmost bound
Of all our fortunes.

A great wound, like losing a limb-
but really, it isn't; his absence seems worse
than it will turn out.Would it have been good
to risk all our forces with a single
throw of the dice?To take such a great gamble
on the chances of one doubtful hour?
It wouldn't be good; for then we could face
absolute defeat, all our hopes
vanishing in one go.

DOUG.
Faith, and so we should;
Where now remains a sweet reversion;
And we may boldly spend upon the hope
Of what is to come in:
A comfort of retirement lives in this.

Indeed, that's right;
now we have something in reserve,
and we can be bold with what we have
knowing we have reserves coming;
if we have to retreat we will have something to fall back on.

HOT.
A rendezvous, a home to fly unto,
If that the Devil and mischance look big
Upon the maidenhead of our affairs.

A meeting place, a place to escape,
if the Devil and bad luck work against
our first efforts.

WOR.
But yet I would your father had been here.
The quality and hair of our attempt
Brooks no division:it will be thought
By some, that know not why he is away,
That wisdom, loyalty, and mere dislike
Of our proceedings, kept the earl from hence:
And think how such an apprehension
May turn the tide of fearful faction,
And breed a kind of question in our cause;
For well you know we of the offering side
Must keep aloof from strict arbitrement,
And stop all sight-holes, every loop from whence
The eye of reason may pry in upon us.
This absence of your father's draws a curtain,
That shows the ignorant a kind of fear
Before not dreamt of.

But I still wish your father was here.
The sort of thing we are attempting
isn't suited to division: it will be thought
by some, who don't know why he is not here,
that wisdom, loyalty, and dislike for
our plans, keep the Earl away:
imagine how such thoughts
might make those who are afraid
run away, questioning our cause;
for you know that we who are attacking
must not think about making judgements,
and keep ourselves from every circumstance
where men can start to think about what they are doing.
Your father's absence draws back the curtain
to show the ignorant a kind of fear
they hadn't imagined before.

HOT.
Nay, you strain too far.
I, rather, of his absence make this use:
It lends a lustre and more great opinion,

A larger dare to our great enterprise,
Than if the earl were here; for men must think,
If we, without his help, can make a head
To push against the kingdom, with his help
We shall o'erturn it topsy-turvy down.
Yet all goes well, yet all our joints are whole.

No, you're making too much of it.
I take his absence to mean this:
it makes our great enterprise more daring,
polishes it, makes men think better of it,
than if the Earl were here; for people will think
that if we, without his help, can start
to unbalance his kingdom, with his help
we can turn the whole thing upside down.
Everything is still going well, we are still unwounded.

DOUG.
As heart can think:there is not such a word
Spoke in Scotland as this term of fear.

All is as well as can be: we don't know
the word fear in Scotland.

[Enter Sir Richard Vernon.]

HOT.
My cousin Vernon! welcome, by my soul.

My cousin Vernon! I give you my warmest welcome.

VER.
Pray God my news be worth a welcome, lord.
The Earl of Westmoreland, seven thousand strong,
Is marching hitherwards; with him Prince John.

I pray to God my news may deserve that welcome, Lord.
The Earl of Westmorland, with seven thousand soldiers,
is marching towards you; Prince John is with him.

HOT.
No harm:what more?

That's not a problem: what else?

VER.
And further, I have learn'd
The King himself in person is set forth,
Or hitherwards intended speedily,
With strong and mighty preparation.

And more, I have learned
that the King himself has set out,
or intends to do so soon,
with a very strong force.

HOT.
He shall be welcome too. Where is his son,
The nimble-footed madcap Prince of Wales,
And his comrades, that daff the world aside,
And bid it pass?

He shall be welcome too. Where is his son,
that swift lunatic Prince of Wales,
and his comrades that reject the world,
letting it pass by them?

VER.
All furnish'd, all in arms;
All plumed like estridges that with the wind
Bate it; like eagles having lately bathed;
Glittering in golden coats, like images;
As full of spirit as the month of May
And gorgeous as the Sun at midsummer;
Wanton as youthful goats, wild as young bulls.
I saw young Harry--with his beaver on,
His cuisses on his thighs, gallantly arm'd--
Rise from the ground like feather'd Mercury,
And vault it with such ease into his seat,
As if an angel dropp'd down from the clouds,
To turn and wind a fiery Pegasus,
And witch the world with noble horsemanship.

They are all ready, they have all taken up arms;
all plumed like ostriches beating their wings against
the wind; like newly bathed eagles;
glittering in golden coats, like statues;
as full of spirit as the month of May

and as gorgeous as the Midsummer sun;
as lusty as young goats, wild as young bulls.
I saw young Harry–with his helmet on,
his thigh armour, strongly armed–
leap from the ground like feathered Mercury,
jumping so easily into his saddle
as if an angel had dropped down from the clouds
to turn and wheel a fiery Pegasus,
and bewitch the whole world with his noble horsemanship.

HOT.
No more, no more:worse than the Sun in March,
This praise doth nourish agues. Let them come;
They come like sacrifices in their trim,
And to the fire-eyed maid of smoky war,
All hot and bleeding, will we offer them:
The mailed Mars shall on his altar sit
Up to the ears in blood. I am on fire
To hear this rich reprisal is so nigh,
And yet not ours.--Come, let me taste my horse,
Who is to bear me, like a thunderbolt,
Against the bosom of the Prince of Wales:
Harry and Harry shall, hot horse to horse,
Meet, and ne'er part till one drop down a corse.--
O, that Glendower were come!

That's enough: your praise causes shudders
worse than the March sun. Let them come;
they come dressed up like sacrifices,
and we shall offer them, hot and bleeding
to the fiery eyed goddess of smoky war:
Mars shall sit on his altar in his armour
up to the ears in blood. I am desperate,
hearing that such a rich prize is nearby
and we haven't taken it.–Come, let me get my horse,
who will carry me, like a thunderbolt,
face-to-face with the Prince of Wales:
Harry and Harry shall meet, horse to horse,
and they won't part until one of them drops down dead.
Oh, I wish Glendower were here!

VER.
There is more news:
I learn'd in Worcester, as I rode along,

He cannot draw his power this fourteen days.

There is more news:
as I came along I learned in Worcester
that he cannot raise his forces within fourteen days.

DOUG.
That's the worst tidings that I hear of yet.

That's the worst news I've heard yet.

WOR.
Ay, by my faith, that bears a frosty sound.

Yes, I swear, that doesn't sound good.

HOT.
What may the King's whole battle reach unto?

What do the whole of the King's forces come to?

VER.
To thirty thousand.

Thirty thousand men.

HOT.
Forty let it be:
My father and Glendower being both away,
The powers of us may serve so great a day.
Come, let us take a muster speedily:
Doomsday is near; die all, die merrily.

Let it be forty thousand:
with my father and Glendower both not being here,
our forces will have to suffice for this great day.
Come, let's get organised quickly:
Doomsday is near; die everyone, die happily.

DOUG.
Talk not of dying:I am out of fear
Of death or death's hand for this one half-year.

Don't talk of dying: I am not worried

about dying within the next six months.

[Exeunt.]

Scene II. A public Road near Coventry.

[Enter Falstaff and Bardolph.]

FAL.
Bardolph, get thee before to Coventry; fill me a bottle of
sack:our soldiers shall march through; we'll to Sutton-Co'fil'
to-night.

*Bardolph, you go ahead to Coventry; get me a bottle of
sack: our soldiers shall march through; we'll be in
Sutton Coldfield tonight.*

BARD.
Will you give me money, captain?

Will you give me the money for it, captain?

FAL.
Lay out, lay out.

Pay for it yourself.

BARD.
This bottle makes an angel.

This bottle means you owe me six shillings.

FAL.
An if it do, take it for thy labour; an if it make twenty,
take them all; I'll answer the coinage. Bid my lieutenant
Peto meet me at the town's end.

*And if I do, take it from expenses; and if it were twenty,
take them all; I'll answer for it. Tell my lieutenant
Peto to meet me the other side of the town.*

BARD.
I will, captain:farewell.

I will, captain: farewell.

[Exit.]

FAL.
If I be not ashamed of my soldiers, I am a soused gurnet. I have
misused the King's press damnably. I have got, in exchange of
a hundred and fifty soldiers, three hundred and odd pounds. I
press'd me none but good householders, yeomen's sons; inquired
me out contracted bachelors, such as had been ask'd twice on the
banns; such a commodity of warm slaves as had as lief hear the
Devil as a drum; such as fear the report of a caliver worse than
a struck fowl or a hurt wild-duck. I press'd me none but such
toasts-and-butter, with hearts in their bodies no bigger than
pins'-heads, and they have bought out their services; and now
my whole charge consists of ancients, corporals, lieutenants,
gentlemen of companies, slaves as ragged as Lazarus in the
painted cloth, where the glutton's dogs licked his sores; and
such as, indeed, were never soldiers, but discarded unjust
serving-men, younger sons to younger brothers, revolted tapsters,
and ostlers trade-fallen; the cankers of a calm world and a long
peace; ten times more dishonourable ragged than an old faced
ancient:and such have I, to fill up the rooms of them that have
bought out their services, that you would think that I had a
hundred and fifty tattered Prodigals lately come from
swine-keeping, from eating draff and husks. A mad fellow met me on
the way, and told me I had unloaded all the gibbets, and press'd
the dead bodies.
No eye hath seen such scarecrows. I'll not march through Coventry
with them, that's flat:nay, and the villains march wide betwixt
the legs, as if they had gyves on; for, indeed, I had the most of
them out of prison. There's but a shirt and a half in all my company;
and the half-shirt is two napkins tack'd together and thrown over the
shoulders like a herald's coat without sleeves; and the shirt, to say
the truth, stolen from my host at Saint Alban's, or the red-nose
innkeeper of Daventry.
But that's all one; they'll find linen enough on every hedge.

If I'm not ashamed of my soldiers, I'm a
pickled fish; I've abused my right of conscription shamefully.
I have got three hundred pounds for a hundred
and fifty soldiers. I've conscripted nobody but
good householders, the sons of Yeomen, I've found
engaged bachelors, who have had their banns read,

such a community of rich slaves who would
just as soon hear the devil as hear the drum,
who fear the sound of gunshots worse than a
wild duck. I conscripted nobody but pampered
citizens, with hearts in their bellies the size of
pinheads, and they have paid to escape service;
and so my entire force consists of old men,
corporals, lieutenants, non-commissioned officers–
slaves as ragged as Lazarus in cheap tapestries,
when the greedy man's dogs licked his sores:
and those who were never soldiers, but dismissed dishonest serving men,
the younger sons of younger brothers, rebellious
barmen, unemployed grooms, the growths of a
calm world and a long piece, ten times more
disreputable than any tattered old flag; and
these are the ones I have to take the places of those who
bought themselves out of service, so you would think that
I had a hundred and fifty ragged wastrels recently
returned from pig keeping, from eating swill and husks.
I met a mad fellow on the way who accused me of
taking down all the hanged men and conscripting the dead bodies.
Nobody's ever seen such scarecrows. I shan't
march through Coventry with them, that's certain: no,
the villains march as if they had chains on their legs,
for it's true I had most of them out of prison.
There isn't a shirt and a half amongst my whole
company, and the half shirt is to napkins tacked together
and thrown over the shoulders like a herald's
coat without sleeves; and to tell the truth the shirt
was stolen from a landlord at St Albans, or the rednosed
innkeeper at Daventry. But it doesn't matter, they can
steal dryinglinen off people's hedges as they pass.

[Enter Prince Henry and Westmoreland.]

PRINCE.
How now, blown Jack! how now, quilt!

Hello there, puffed out Jack! Hello there, quilt!

FAL.
What, Hal! how now, mad wag! what a devil dost thou in
Warwickshire?--My good Lord of Westmoreland, I cry you mercy:
I thought your honour had already been at Shrewsbury.

What, Hal! Hello there, mad lad! What the devil are you doing in
Warwickshire? My good Lord of Westmorland, excuse me:
I thought your honour was already at Shrewsbury.

WEST.
Faith, Sir John, 'tis more than time that I were there, and you too;
but my powers are there already. The King, I can tell you, looks for
us all:we must away all, to-night.

I swear, St John, it's about time that I was there, and you too;
but my forces are already there. The King, I can tell you, is waiting for
all of us: we must all leave, tonight.

FAL.
Tut, never fear me:I am as vigilant as a cat to steal cream.

Tut, don't worry about me: I am as keen as a cat waiting to steal cream.

PRINCE.
I think, to steal cream, indeed; for thy theft hath already made thee
butter. But tell me, Jack, whose fellows are these that come after?

Stealing cream indeed, for your theft has already made you
into butter. But tell me, Jack, whose are these men following?

FAL.
Mine, Hal, mine.

Mine, Hal, mine.

PRINCE.
I did never see such pitiful rascals.

I never saw such pitiful rascals.

FAL.
Tut, tut; good enough to toss; food for powder, food for powder;
they'll fill a pit as well as better:tush, man, mortal men,
mortal men.

Tut-tut; they're good enough to throw in; cannon fodder, cannon fodder;
they'll fill a grave as well as the next man: mortal men,
mortal men.

WEST.
Ay, but, Sir John, methinks they are exceeding poor and bare,--too
beggarly.

*Yes, but, Sir John, they seem to me extremely poor and badly turned out–
they are like beggars.*

FAL.
Faith, for their poverty, I know not where they had that; and,
for their bareness, I am sure they never learn'd that of me.

*Well, I swear I don't know how they got poor; and
as for their turnout, I'm sure they didn't learn that from me.*

PRINCE.
No, I'll be sworn; unless you call three fingers on the ribs
bare. But, sirrah, make haste:Percy is already in the field.

*No, I'll swear to that; unless you say three fingers of fat
on the chest is a good turnout. But, sir, hurry: Percy is already on the battlefield.*

[Exit.]

FAL.
What, is the King encamp'd?

What, has the King set up camp?

WEST.
He is, Sir John:I fear we shall stay too long.

He has, Sir John: I fear we will be late.

[Exit.]

FAL.
Well,
To the latter end of a fray and the beginning of a feast
Fits a dull fighter and a keen guest.

*Well,
it suits a reluctant fighter and a keen eater
to arrive at the end of the battle and the beginning of the feast.*

[Exit.]

Scene III. The Rebel Camp near Shrewsbury.

[Enter Hotspur, Worcester, Douglas, and Vernon.]

HOT.
We'll fight with him to-night.

We'll fight with him tonight.

WOR.
It may not be.

We may not.

DOUG.
You give him, then, advantage.

Then you'll hand him the advantage.

VER.
Not a whit.

Not at all.

HOT.
Why say you so? looks he not for supply?

Why do you say so? Isn't he waiting for reinforcements?

VER.
So do we.

We are too.

HOT.
His is certain, ours is doubtful.

He can rely on his, we can't on ours.

WOR.

Good cousin, be advised; stir not to-night.

Good cousin, take my advice; don't move tonight.

VER.
Do not, my lord.

Don't, my lord.

DOUG.
You do not counsel well:
You speak it out of fear and cold heart.

This is not good advice:
you're giving it from fear and cowardice.

VER.
Do me no slander, Douglas:by my life,--
And I dare well maintain it with my life,--
If well-respected honour bid me on,
I hold as little counsel with weak fear
As you, my lord, or any Scot that this day lives:
Let it be seen to-morrow in the battle
Which of us fears.

Don't badmouth me, Douglas: on my life–
and I will back it up with my life–
if a well-respected honourable man orders me on,
I will have as little truck with weak fear
as you, my lord, or any Scot alive:
let's see in the battle tomorrow
which of us is afraid.

DOUG.
Yea, or to-night.

Yes, or tonight.

VER.
Content.

Enough.

HOT.

To-night, say I.

I say tonight.

VER.
Come, come, it may not be. I wonder much,
Being men of such great leading as you are,
That you foresee not what impediments
Drag back our expedition:certain Horse
Of my cousin Vernon's are not yet come up:
Your uncle Worcester's Horse came but to-day;
And now their pride and mettle is asleep,
Their courage with hard labour tame and dull,
That not a horse is half the half himself.

Come, come, it can't happen. I'm astonished
that men who are such great leaders
can't see the drawbacks to
your plan: some cavalry
of my cousin Vernon's haven't arrived:
the cavalry of your uncle Worcester only came today;
and now all their brave horses are asleep,
their courage dulled by their hard labour,
so no horse is a quarter of himself.

HOT.
So are the horses of the enemy
In general, journey-bated and brought low:
The better part of ours are full of rest.

And most of the enemy's horses
are worn out with their journey as well:
the greater part ofours are well rested.

WOR.
The number of the King exceedeth ours.
For God's sake, cousin, stay till all come in.

The King has greater numbers than us.
For God's sake, cousin, wait until we have them all here.

[The Trumpet sounds a parley.]

[Enter Sir Walter Blunt.]

BLUNT.
I come with gracious offers from the King,
If you vouchsafe me hearing and respect.

I come with generous offers from the King,
if you will give me a respectful hearing.

HOT.
Welcome, Sir Walter Blunt; and would to God
You were of our determination!
Some of us love you well; and even those some
Envy your great deservings and good name,
Because you are not of our quality,
But stand against us like an enemy.

Welcome, Sir Walter Blunt; I wish to God
that you were on our side!
Some of us love you very much; and they
envy your great reputation and good name,
because you are not on our side,
but stand against us like an enemy.

BLUNT.
And God defend but still I should stand so,
So long as out of limit and true rule
You stand against anointed majesty!
But to my charge:the King hath sent to know
The nature of your griefs; and whereupon
You conjure from the breast of civil peace
Such bold hostility, teaching his duteous land
Audacious cruelty. If that the King
Have any way your good deserts forgot,
Which he confesseth to be manifold,
He bids you name your griefs; and with all speed
You shall have your desires with interest,
And pardon absolute for yourself and these
Herein misled by your suggestion.

And God forfend that I should stand otherwise,
as long as you wrongly rebel
against anointed majesty!
But this is my task: the King has sent me to ask
what is the nature of your complaints; and why

you have conjured up such terrible war
from the peaceful country, showing daring cruelty
to his loyal land. If the King
has in any way neglected to reward your good
qualities, which he admits are many,
he asks you to name your grievances; and at once
you shall have what you ask for and more,
with a complete pardon for yourself and those
who have been led astray by you.

HOT.
The King is kind; and well we know the King
Knows at what time to promise, when to pay.
My father and my uncle and myself
Did give him that same royalty he wears;
And--when he was not six-and-twenty strong,
Sick in the world's regard, wretched and low,
A poor unminded outlaw sneaking home--
My father gave him welcome to the shore:
And--when he heard him swear and vow to God,
He came but to be Duke of Lancaster,
To sue his livery and beg his peace,
With tears of innocence and terms of zeal--
My father, in kind heart and pity moved,
Swore him assistance, and performed it too.
Now, when the lords and barons of the realm
Perceived Northumberland did lean to him,
The more and less came in with cap and knee;
Met him in boroughs, cities, villages,
Attended him on bridges, stood in lanes,
Laid gifts before him, proffer'd him their oaths,
Give him their heirs as pages, follow'd him
Even at the heels in golden multitudes.
He presently--as greatness knows itself--
Steps me a little higher than his vow
Made to my father, while his blood was poor,
Upon the naked shore at Ravenspurg;
And now, forsooth, takes on him to reform
Some certain edicts and some strait decrees
That lie too heavy on the commonwealth;
Cries out upon abuses, seems to weep
Over his country's wrongs; and, by this face,
This seeming brow of justice, did he win
The hearts of all that he did angle for:

Proceeded further; cut me off the heads
Of all the favourites, that the absent King
In deputation left behind him here
When he was personal in the Irish war.

The King is kind, and we know well that the King
knows what time to make promises, and when to pay:
my father, and my uncle, and myself
gave him the kingship he enjoys now
when he had just twenty six soldiers,
had no standing in the world, was wretched and low,
a poor unnoticed outlaw sneaking home,
my father welcomed him to the shore:
and when he heard him swear and vow to God
that he only wanted to be Duke of Lancaster,
to reclaim his lands, and ask for peace
with innocent tears, and great passion,
my father, moved by pity and being kind
swore to help him, and kept his promise.
Now, when the Lords and barons of the kingdom
saw that Northumberland favoured him,
both high and low came to pay respects,
met him in boroughs, cities, villages,
waited for him on bridges, stood in lanes,
gave him presents, swore loyalty to him,
gave him their heirs as servants, followed him
closely in magnificent crowds.
Soon after, thinking himself to be great,
he advanced a little higher than the vow
he made to my father when he was low
on the bare shore at Ravenspurgh;
and then, by God, he decided to reform
certain laws and taxes
which were lying too heavily on the country;
he spoke out against abuses, seemed to weep
over the wrongs done to his country; and by pretending
that he was acting for justice he won over
the hearts of everyone he wanted;
then he went further–he cut off the heads
of all the favourites that the absent King
had left behind as his deputies,
when he went to the war in Ireland.

BLUNT.

170

Tut, I came not to hear this.

Tut, I didn't come to listen to this.

HOT.
Then to the point:
In short time after, he deposed the King;
Soon after that, deprived him of his life;
And, in the neck of that, task'd the whole State:
To make that worse, suffer'd his kinsman March
(Who is, if every owner were well placed,
Indeed his king) to be engaged in Wales,
There without ransom to lie forfeited;
Disgraced me in my happy victories,
Sought to entrap me by intelligence;
Rated my uncle from the Council-board;
In rage dismiss'd my father from the Court;
Broke oath on oath, committed wrong on wrong;
And, in conclusion, drove us to seek out
This head of safety; and withal to pry
Into his title, the which now we find
Too indirect for long continuance.

Then I'll get to the point:
a short time after, he overthrew the king;
soon after that, he took away his life;
and at once he began taxing the whole country:
to make it worse, he allowed his kinsman Mortimer
(who, if everyone were in their right place,
would be King) to be held as hostage in Wales,
to live there abandoned without ransom;
he put a disgraceful spin on my great victories,
and tried to trap me with his spies,
attacked my uncle in the council,
angrily dismissed my father from the court,
broke oath after oath, committed wrong after wrong,
and in the end forced us to raise
this army for our defence, and also to
question his right to be king, and we find
that his claim is too tenuous to be upheld.

BLUNT.
Shall I return this answer to the King?

Shall I take this answer back to the King?

HOT.
Not so, Sir Walter:we'll withdraw awhile.
Go to the King; and let there be impawn'd
Some surety for a safe return again,
And in the morning early shall my uncle
Bring him our purposes: and so, farewell.

No, Sir Walter: we'll withdraw for a while.
Go to the King; let him give guarantees
that anyone coming from me will be safe,
and early in the morning my uncle will
bring him news of our intentions: and so, farewell.

BLUNT.
I would you would accept of grace and love.

I wish you would accept grace and love.

HOT.
And may be so we shall.

Maybe we will.

BLUNT.
Pray God you do.

I pray to God that you do.

[Exeunt.]

Scene IV. York.A Room in the Archbishop's Palace.

[Enter the Archbishop of York and Sir Michael.]

ARCH.
Hie, good Sir Michael; bear this sealed brief
With winged haste to the Lord Marshal;
This to my cousin Scroop; and all the rest
To whom they are directed. If you knew
How much they do import, you would make haste.

Go, good sir Michael; take this sealed letter
as fast as you can to the Lord Marshall;
this one to my cousin Scroop; and all the rest
as they are addressed. If you knew
how important they are, you would hurry.

SIR M.
My good lord,
I guess their tenour.

My good lord,
I can guess their content.

ARCH.
Like enough you do.
To-morrow, good Sir Michael, is a day
Wherein the fortune of ten thousand men
Must bide the touch; for, sir, at Shrewsbury,
As I am truly given to understand,
The King, with mighty and quick-raised power,
Meets with Lord Harry:and, I fear, Sir Michael,
What with the sickness of Northumberland,
Whose power was in the first proportion,
And what with Owen Glendower's absence thence,
Who with them was a rated sinew too,
And comes not in, o'er-rul'd by prophecies,--
I fear the power of Percy is too weak
To wage an instant trial with the King.

I expect you can.
Tomorrow, good Sir Michael, is a day
when the fate of ten thousand men will be
put to the test; for, sir, at Shrewsbury,
I have been given to understand,
the King, with great and swiftly gathered forces,
meets with Lord Harry: and I fear, Sir Michael,
that with the sickness of Northumberland,
who had the greatest share of power,
and what with Owen Glendower's absence,
he was a great part of their strength as well,
and he has not arrived, believing in prophecies–
I fear the power of Percy is too weak
to take on a fight with the King at the moment.

SIR M.
Why, my good lord, you need not fear;
There's Douglas and Lord Mortimer.

Why, my good lord, you need not be afraid;
he has Douglas and Lord Mortimer.

ARCH.
No, Mortimer's not there.

No, Mortimer is not there.

SIR M.
But there is Mordake, Vernon, Lord Harry Percy,
And there's my Lord of Worcester; and a head
Of gallant warriors, noble gentlemen.

But there is Mordake, Vernon, Lord Harry Percy,
and my Lord of Worcester; and a force
of gallant warriors, noble gentlemen.

ARCH.
And so there is:but yet the King hath drawn
The special head of all the land together;
The Prince of Wales, Lord John of Lancaster,
The noble Westmoreland, and warlike Blunt;
And many more corrivals and dear men
Of estimation and command in arms.

That's true: but still the king has gathered
the greatest forces in the land together;
the Prince of Wales, Lord John of Lancaster,
the noble Westmorland, and warlike Blunt;
and many more associates and good men
of good reputation as fighters.

SIR M.
Doubt not, my lord, they shall be well opposed.

Do not think, my lord, that they won't be strongly opposed.

ARCH.
I hope no less, yet needful 'tis to fear;
And, to prevent the worst, Sir Michael, speed:
For if Lord Percy thrive not, ere the King
Dismiss his power, he means to visit us,
For he hath heard of our confederacy;
And 'tis but wisdom to make strong against him:
Therefore make haste. I must go write again
To other friends; and so, farewell, Sir Michael.

That's what I hope, but caution is necessary;
and, to prevent the worst happening, Sir Michael, hurry:
for if Lord Percy does not succeed, the King
intends to attack us before he dissolves his army,
for he has heard about our Alliance;
it's only sensible to prepare defences against him:
so hurry. I must go and write more
to other friends; and so, farewell, Sir Michael.

[Exeunt.]

Act V

Scene I. The King's Camp near Shrewsbury.

[Enter King Henry, Prince Henry, Lancaster, Sir Walter Blunt,
and Sir John Falstaff.]

KING.
How bloodily the Sun begins to peer
Above yon bulky hill! the day looks pale
At his distemperature.

How bloody the sun looks peering
over that great hill! The day looks pale
at his illness.

PRINCE.
The southern wind
Doth play the trumpet to his purposes;
And by his hollow whistling in the leaves
Foretells a tempest and a blustering day.

The southern wind
is playing his own tune;
his hollow whistling through the leaves
predicts a storm and a windy day.

KING.
Then with the losers let it sympathize,
For nothing can seem foul to those that win.--

[The trumpet sounds. Enter Worcester and Vernon.]

How, now, my Lord of Worcester! 'tis not well
That you and I should meet upon such terms
As now we meet. You have deceived our trust;
And made us doff our easy robes of peace,
To crush our old limbs in ungentle steel:
This is not well, my lord, this is not well.
What say you to't? will you again unknit
This churlish knot of all-abhorred war,
And move in that obedient orb again

Where you did give a fair and natural light;
And be no more an exhaled meteor,
A prodigy of fear, and a portent
Of broached mischief to the unborn times?

Then let it suit the mood of the losers,
for nothing can look bad to those who win-

Hello, my lord of Worcester!It's not good
that you and I should meet on these terms.
You have betrayed my trust,
and made me remove the soft clothes of peace,
to crush my old limbs into harsh steel armour:
this is not good, my lord, this is not good.
What have you to say about it? Will you untie
this horrid knot of hated war,
and come back into the orbit of the planet
which gave you a fair natural light;
stop being a riotous meteor, a
bringer of fear, and a sign of
terrible harm to future ages?

WOR.
Hear me, my liege:
For mine own part, I could be well content
To entertain the lag-end of my life
With quiet hours; for I do protest,
I have not sought the day of this dislike.

Hear me, my lord:
for my part, I would be very glad
to spend my last years quietly;
I must point out that I
didn't look for this day of conflict.

KING.
You have not sought it! why, how comes it, then?

You didn't look for it!How's it happened then?

FAL.
Rebellion lay in his way, and he found it.

He came across rebellion, and picked it up.

178

PRINCE.
Peace, chewet, peace!

Peace, chatterer, be quiet!

WOR.
It pleased your Majesty to turn your looks
Of favour from myself and all our House;
And yet I must remember you, my lord,
We were the first and dearest of your friends.
For you my staff of office did I break
In Richard's time; and posted day and night
To meet you on the way, and kiss your hand,
When yet you were in place and in account
Nothing so strong and fortunate as I.
It was myself, my brother, and his son,
That brought you home, and boldly did outdare
The dangers of the time. You swore to us,--
And you did swear that oath at Doncaster,--
That you did nothing purpose 'gainst the state;
Nor claim no further than your new-fall'n right,
The seat of Gaunt, dukedom of Lancaster:
To this we swore our aid. But in short space
It rain'd down fortune showering on your head;
And such a flood of greatness fell on you,--
What with our help, what with the absent King,
What with the injuries of a wanton time,
The seeming sufferances that you had borne,
And the contrarious winds that held the King
So long in his unlucky Irish wars
That all in England did repute him dead,--
And, from this swarm of fair advantages,
You took occasion to be quickly woo'd
To gripe the general sway into your hand;
Forgot your oath to us at Doncaster;
And, being fed by us, you used us so
As that ungentle gull, the cuckoo-bird,
Useth the sparrow; did oppress our nest;
Grew by our feeding to so great a bulk,
That even our love durst not come near your sight
For fear of swallowing; but with nimble wing
We were enforced, for safety-sake, to fly
Out of your sight, and raise this present head:

Whereby we stand opposed by such means
As you yourself have forged against yourself,
By unkind usage, dangerous countenance,
And violation of all faith and troth
Sworn to us in your younger enterprise.

Your Majesty decided that I and all my family
were out of favour;
I must remind you, my lord,
that we were your oldest and closest friends.
I threw away my job as steward for you
in Richard's time; I rode night and day
to meet you on the journey, and kiss your hand,
when you didn't have anything like
my fame or position.
It was I, my brother and my son
who brought you home, boldly risking
the dangers of the time. You swore to us -
you swore the oath at Doncaster -
that you had no intentions against the country;
you said all you wanted was your newly-inherited title,
the seat of Gaunt, the dukedom of Gloucester:
we swore to help you in that. But very swiftly
a great fortune fell down upon your head,
a huge flood of greatness -
with our help, with the king absent,
with the hardships of that wild time,
the hardships you seemed to have suffered,
and the unfavourable winds which kept the King
stuck for so long in his unlucky Irish wars
that everyone in England believed he was dead -
with all this good luck
you allowed yourself to be quickly persuaded
to take power into your hands;
you forgot what you had sworn to us at Doncaster;
and, having been helped by us, you were like
that ungrateful bird the cuckoo; you filled our nest,
became so huge from our feeding you
that even we who loved you dared not come near
for fear of being swallowed; we were forced
for our safety to flee from you and raise these forces:
so we are opposing you with weapons
you have created against yourself,
through unkind treatment, threatening behaviour,

and violation of all the oaths and promises
you made to us in those early days.

KING.
These things, indeed, you have articulate,
Proclaim'd at market-crosses, read in churches,
To face the garment of rebellion
With some fine colour that may please the eye
Of fickle changelings and poor discontents,
Which gape and rub the elbow at the news
Of hurlyburly innovation:
And never yet did insurrection want
Such water-colours to impaint his cause;
Nor moody beggars, starving for a time
Of pellmell havoc and confusion.

These are the things that you have mentioned,
announced at market crosses, read out in churches,
to dress up the clothes of rebellion
with some lovely colour to please the eye
of fickle changeable people and poor malcontents,
who gape and jostle at the news
of any new disturbance;
no rebellion ever lacked
this type of excuse to dress up its cause,
or sullen beggars eager for a time
of riot and confusion.

PRINCE.
In both our armies there is many a soul
Shall pay full dearly for this encounter,
If once they join in trial. Tell your nephew,
The Prince of Wales doth join with all the world
In praise of Henry Percy:by my hopes,
This present enterprise set off his head,
I do not think a braver gentleman,
More active-valiant or more valiant-young,
More daring or more bold, is now alive
To grace this latter age with noble deeds.
For my part,--I may speak it to my shame,--
I have a truant been to chivalry;
And so I hear he doth account me too:
Yet this before my father's Majesty,--
I am content that he shall take the odds

Of his great name and estimation,
And will, to save the blood on either side,
Try fortune with him in a single fight.

There are many souls in both our armies
who will pay the ultimate price for our battle,
once it begins.Tell your nephew
that the Prince of Wales praises Henry Percy
like the rest of the world; it's my opinion,
discounting this current business,
that there isn't a braver gentleman,
more active - braver or less brave -
more daring or bold currently alive
to grace this current age with noble deeds.
For my part - I say it with shame-
I have been a stranger to chivalry;
and I've heard he thinks the same:
but I swear this before my royal father,
that I am happy for him to bring
his great name and fame and,
to save bloodshed on both sides,
to try my luck with him in single combat.

KING.
And, Prince of Wales, so dare we venture thee,
Albeit considerations infinite
Do make against it.--No, good Worcester, no;
We love our people well; even those we love
That are misled upon your cousin's part;
And, will they take the offer of our grace,
Both he, and they, and you, yea, every man
Shall be my friend again, and I'll be his:
So tell your cousin, and then bring me word
What he will do:but, if he will not yield,
Rebuke and dread correction wait on us,
And they shall do their office. So, be gone;
We will not now be troubled with reply:
We offer fair; take it advisedly.

And, Prince of Wales, I am prepared to risk you,
even though there are many great reasons
not to do it.No, good Worcester, no;
I love my people well; I love even those
who have been misled by your cousin;

182

and, if they will accept my offer of pardon,
both he, and they, and you, yes, every man,
will be my friend again, and I shall be his:
tell your cousin this, and then bring me word
of what he will do: but, if he won't back down,
a terrible vengeance will be their punishment.
So, go; I don't want an answer now:
it's a fair offer; you'd be wise to consider it.

[Exit Worcester with Vernon.]

PRINCE.
It will not be accepted, on my life:
The Douglas and the Hotspur both together
Are confident against the world in arms.

I swear they won't accept it:
Douglas and Hotspur together
back themselves against anyone in a fight.

KING.
Hence, therefore, every leader to his charge;
For, on their answer, will we set on them:
And God befriend us, as our cause is just!

So, every leader must go to his forces;
once we have their answer we shall attack,
and may God help us, as our cause is just!

[Exeunt the King, Blunt, and Prince John.]

FAL.
Hal, if thou see me down in the battle, and bestride me,
so; 'tis a point of friendship.

Hal, if you see me fall in battle then stand over me;
that's what a friend should do.

PRINCE.
Nothing but a colossus can do thee that friendship.
Say thy prayers, and farewell.

Only a giant could stand over you.
Say your prayers, and good luck.

FAL.
I would it were bedtime, Hal, and all well.

I wish it was bedtime, Hal, and everything was settled.

PRINCE.
Why, thou owest God a death.

Well, you owe God a death.

[Exit.]

FAL.
'Tis not due yet; I would be loth to pay Him before His day.
What need I be so forward with him that calls not on me?
Well, 'tis no matter; honour pricks me on. Yea, but how if honour
prick me off when I come on? how then? Can honor set-to a leg?
no:or an arm? no:or take away the grief of a wound? no. Honour
hath no skill in surgery then? no. What is honour? a word. What
is that word, honour? air. A trim reckoning!--Who hath it? he that
died o' Wednesday. Doth he feel it? no. Doth be hear it? no. Is it
insensible, then? yea, to the dead. But will it not live with the
living? no. Why? detraction will not suffer it. Therefore I'll none
of it:honour is a mere scutcheon:--and so ends my catechism.

It's not due yet; I don't want to pay Him before the day comes.
Why should I offer before He asks for it?
Well, no matter; honour spurs me on. Yes, but what if honour
gets stuck into me when I go on? Can honour reattach a leg?
No: or an arm? No: or take away the pain of a wound? No. Has
honour any skill in surgery? No. What is honour? A word. What
is that word, honour? Breath. A heavy price! Who has it? Someone
who died on Wednesday. Can he feel it? No? Does he hear it? No. Is it useless, then? Yes, to the
dead. But won't it stay with the living? No.
Why not? It won't stand up to criticism. So I want nothing to do
with it. Honour is just a dressing for a coffin: that's my opinion.

[Exit.]

Scene II. The Rebel Camp.

[Enter Worcester and Vernon.]

WOR.
O no, my nephew must not know, Sir Richard,
The liberal-kind offer of the King.

Oh no, Sir Richard, we mustn't let my nephew know
this generous kind offer from the King.

VER.
'Twere best he did.

It's best he does.

WOR.
Then are we all undone.
It is not possible, it cannot be,
The King should keep his word in loving us;
He will suspect us still, and find a time
To punish this offence in other faults:
Suspicion all our lives shall be stuck full of eyes;
For treason is but trusted like the fox,
Who, ne'er so tame, so cherish'd, and lock'd up,
Will have a wild trick of his ancestors.
Look how we can, or sad or merrily,
Interpretation will misquote our looks;
And we shall feed like oxen at a stall,
The better cherish'd, still the nearer death.
My nephew's trespass may be well forgot:
It hath th' excuse of youth and heat of blood,
And an adopted name of privilege,--
A hare-brain'd Hotspur, govern'd by a spleen:
All his offences live upon my head
And on his father's:we did train him on;
And, his corruption being ta'en from us,
We, as the spring of all, shall pay for all.
Therefore, good cousin, let not Harry know,
In any case, the offer of the King.

Then we are all lost.
It isn't possible, it can't happen,
that the King would keep his word to love us;
he will still suspect us, and find a time
to punish our offences in other ways:
we will always be looked at with suspicion,
for treason can only be trusted like a fox,
who, however tame, however loved and domesticated,
will always retain his wild side.
However we look, sad or happy,
we will be misinterpreted,
and we will be like oxen feeding in a stall,
more pampered the nearer we get to death.
My nephew's rebellion might well be forgotten,
excused by his youth and his passion,
and a nickname which allows him to be rash–
harebrained Hotspur, governed by spleen:
all his offences will fall on the head of me
and his father. We encouraged him,
and, having been led astray by us,
we as the instigators will pay for everything:
therefore, good cousin, do not let Harry know
the offer of the King under any circumstances.

VER.
Deliver what you will, I'll say 'tis so.
Here comes your cousin.

Say what you want, I shall back you.
Here comes your cousin.

[Enter Hotspur and Douglas; Officers and Soldiers behind.]

HOT.
My uncle is return'd: deliver up
My Lord of Westmoreland.--Uncle, what news?

My uncle has come back: bring me
my Lord of Westmorland. Uncle, what's the news?

WOR.
The King will bid you battle presently.

The King will invite you to battle soon.

DOUG.
Defy him by the Lord Of Westmoreland.

Send a message of defiance by the Lord of Westmorland.

HOT.
Lord Douglas, go you and tell him so.

Lord Douglas, you go and tell him so.

DOUG.
Marry, I shall, and very willingly.

I certainly shall, very willingly.

[Exit.]

WOR.
There is no seeming mercy in the King.

It seems the king has no mercy.

HOT.
Did you beg any? God forbid!

Did you beg for any? Heaven forbid!

WOR.
I told him gently of our grievances,
Of his oath-breaking; which he mended thus,
By new-forswearing that he is forsworn:
He calls us rebels, traitors; and will scourge
With haughty arms this hateful name in us.

I told him politely of our grievances,
about his oath breaking; he answered
with yet another false oath:
he calls us rebels, traitors; and he will tear
at our hated name with his arrogant forces.

[Re-enter Douglas.]

DOUG.

Arm, gentlemen; to arms! for I have thrown
A brave defiance in King Henry's teeth,
And Westmoreland, that was engaged, did bear it;
Which cannot choose but bring him quickly on.

*Arm yourselves, gentlemen; arm yourselves! I have thrown
brave defiance back in King Henry's face,
and Westmorland has taken it to him as I ordered;
that can't help but bring him on quickly.*

WOR.

The Prince of Wales stepp'd forth before the King,
And, nephew, challenged you to single fight.

*The Prince of Wales stepped out ahead of the King,
and, nephew, challenged you to single combat.*

HOT.

O, would the quarrel lay upon our heads;
And that no man might draw short breath to-day
But I and Harry Monmouth! Tell me, tell me,
How show'd his tasking? seem'd it in contempt?

*Oh, I would like for just the two of us to fight,
so that no man today would fight apart from
me and Harry Monmouth! Tell me, tell me,
what was his challenge like? Did it seem contemptuous?*

VER.

No, by my soul: I never in my life
Did hear a challenge urged more modestly,
Unless a brother should a brother dare
To gentle exercise and proof of arms.
He gave you all the duties of a man;
Trimm'd up your praises with a princely tongue;
Spoke your deservings like a chronicle;
Making you ever better than his praise,
By still dispraising praise valued with you;
And, which became him like a prince indeed,
He made a blushing cital of himself;
And chid his truant youth with such a grace,
As if he master'd there a double spirit,
Of teaching and of learning instantly.

There did he pause:but let me tell the world,
If he outlive the envy of this day,
England did never owe so sweet a hope,
So much misconstrued in his wantonness.

No, I swear: I never in my life
Heard a more modest challenge,
it was like a brother challenging a brother
to a gentle fencing match.
He acknowledged all your virtues as a man;
he richly praised you with a princely tongue;
he spoke of your reputation like a history book;
he made you seem even greater than his praise,
by saying that his praises could not do you justice;
and, what was very princely of him,
he made a very modest assessment of himself;
he criticised his wasted youth with such grace,
as if he had managed the trick of
teaching and learning simultaneously.
He paused there there: but let me tell the world—
if he survives the evils of this day,
England never had such a great hope
who has been so misunderstood through his behaviour.

HOT.
Cousin, I think thou art enamoured
Upon his follies: never did I hear
Of any prince so wild o' liberty.
But be he as he will, yet once ere night
I will embrace him with a soldier's arm,
That he shall shrink under my courtesy.--
Arm, arm with speed:and, fellows, soldiers, friends,
Better consider what you have to do
Than I, that have not well the gift of tongue,
Can lift your blood up with persuasion.

Cousin, you seem to be charmed
by his foolishness: I never heard
of any prince who was such a libertine.
But whatever he's like, before nightfall
I will give him the embrace of a soldier,
and he shall fall down from my affection.
Arm yourselves, quickly: and, fellows, soldiers, friends,
think of what you have to do, you can

do that better for yourselves, I don't have
the gift of the gab to get you going.

[Enter a Messenger.]

MESS.
My lord, here are letters for you.

My Lord, here are letters for you.

HOT.
I cannot read them now.--
O gentlemen, the time of life is short!
To spend that shortness basely were too long,
If life did ride upon a dial's point,
Still ending at th' arrival of an hour.
An if we live, we live to tread on kings;
If die, brave death, when princes die with us!
Now, for our consciences, the arms are fair,
When the intent of bearing them is just.

I cannot read them now.
Oh gentlemen, life is short!
If life was just an hour long
it would still be too long if it was not
spent wisely.
If we live, we live to triumph over Kings,
if we die, what a good death when princes die with us!
We can fight with good conscience
knowing that our intentions are pure.

[Enter another Messenger.]

MESS.
My lord, prepare:the King comes on apace.

My Lord, get ready: the King is approaching quickly.

HOT.
I thank him, that he cuts me from my tale,
For I profess not talking; only this,
Let each man do his best:and here draw I
A sword, whose temper I intend to stain
With the best blood that I can meet withal

190

In the adventure of this perilous day.
Now, Esperance! Percy! and set on.
Sound all the lofty instruments of war,
And by that music let us all embrace;
For, Heaven to Earth, some of us never shall
A second time do such a courtesy.

I thank him for stopping my speech,
for I am not a good talker; I'll just say this,
let every man do his best: and here I draw
a sword, whose steel I intend to stain
with the best blood that I can find
on this dangerous day.
Now, cry Hope! Percy! And set to.
Play all the great instruments of war,
and let us all embrace tothat music;
for it's odds-on that some of us will never
have a chance to do this again.

[The trumpets sound.They embrace, and exeunt.]

Scene III. Plain between the Camps.

[Excursions, and Parties fighting.Alarum to the battle.
Then enter Douglas and Sir Walter Blunt, meeting.]

BLUNT.
What is thy name, that in the battle thus
Thou crossest me? what honour dost thou seek
Upon my head?

What is your name, you who crosses me
in battle? What honour do you seek
by taking my head?

DOUG.
Know, then, my name is Douglas,
And I do haunt thee in the battle thus
Because some tell me that thou art a king.

I tell you that my name is Douglas,
and I am pursuing you in the battle
because I have been told that you are a king.

BLUNT.
They tell thee true.

You have heard right.

DOUG.
The Lord of Stafford dear to-day hath bought
Thy likeness; for, instead of thee, King Harry,
This sword hath ended him:so shall it thee,
Unless thou yield thee as my prisoner.

The Lord of Stafford paid a high price today for
looking like you; for, instead of you, King Harry,
this sword killed him: it shall do the same to you,
unless you surrender as my prisoner.

BLUNT.

I was not born a yielder, thou proud Scot;
And thou shalt find a king that will revenge
Lord Stafford's death.

I was not born to surrender, you proud Scot;
and you will find a king who will avenge
Lord Stafford's death.

[They fight, and Blunt is slain. Enter Hotspur.]

HOT.
O Douglas, hadst thou fought at Holmedon thus,
I never had triumphed o'er a Scot.

Oh Douglas, if you had fought like this at Holmedon
I would never have beaten a single Scot.

DOUG.
All's done, all's won; here breathless lies the King.

It's over, we've won; here lies the King, dead.

HOT.
Where?

Where?

DOUG.
Here.

Here.

HOT.
This, Douglas? no; I know this face full well:
A gallant knight he was, his name was Blunt;
Semblably furnish'd like the King himself.

This, Douglas? No; I recognise this man:
he was a gallant knight, he was called Blunt;
he is dressed the same as the King.

DOUG.
A fool go with thy soul, where're it goes!
A borrow'd title hast thou bought too dear:

Why didst thou tell me that thou wert a king?

May you be called a fool, wherever your soul goes!
You have paid too dearly for that borrowed title:
why did you tell me that you were a king?

HOT.
The King hath many marching in his coats.

The King has many soldiers wearing his uniform.

DOUG.
Now, by my sword, I will kill all his coats;
I'll murder all his wardrobe piece by piece,
Until I meet the King.

I swear by my sword I'll kill all his uniforms;
I'll murder his wardrobe piece by piece,
until I meet the King.

HOT.
Up, and away!
Our soldiers stand full fairly for the day.

Up, and away!
Our soldiers are fully engaged.

[Exeunt.]

[Alarums. Enter Falstaff.]

FAL.
Though I could 'scape shot-free at London, I fear the shot
here; here's no scoring but upon the pate.--Soft! who are you?
Sir Walter Blunt:there's honour for you! here's no vanity! I am
as hot as molten lead, and as heavy too:God keep lead out of me!
I need no more weight than mine own bowels. I have led my
ragamuffins where they are peppered:there's not three of my
hundred and fifty left alive; and they are for the town's end, to
beg during life. But who comes here?

I could have stayed out of range in London, I fear the
shooting here; our heads are the only targets. Wait! Who are you?
Sir Walter Blunt: that's what honour gets you! No vanity here! I am

194

as hot as molten lead, and as heavy too: may God keep lead out of me!
I don't need any more ballast than my own stomach. I have led my
ragamuffins into dangerous places: there are not three of my
hundred and fifty left alive; and they will end up begging on the
outskirts of town. But who's this?

[Enter Prince Henry.]

PRINCE.
What, stand'st thou idle here? lend me thy sword:
Many a nobleman lies stark and stiff
Under the hoofs of vaunting enemies,
Whose deaths are yet unrevenged:I pr'ythee,
Lend me thy sword.

What, are you standing here doing nothing? Lend me your sword:
there are many noblemen lying stiff and cold
under the hooves of their proud enemies,
whose deaths have not yet been revenged: I beg you,
lend me your sword.

FAL.
O Hal, I pr'ythee give me leave to breathe awhile. Turk
Gregory never did such deeds in arms as I have done this
day. I have paid Percy, I have made him sure.

Oh Hal, please give me time to catch my breath.
The angry Gregory never performed such feats of arms as
I have today. I have killed Percy, I have made sure of him.

PRINCE.
He is indeed; and living to kill thee.
I pr'ythee, lend me thy sword.

It's certainly sure that he's still alive to kill you.
Please, lend me your sword.

FAL.
Nay, before God, Hal, if Percy be alive, thou gett'st not
my sword; but take my pistol, if thou wilt.

No, I swear, Hal, if Percy is alive, you're not getting
my sword; but take my pistol, if you want.

PRINCE.
Give it me:what, is it in the case?

Give it to me: what, is it in its holster?

FAL.
Ay, Hal. 'Tis hot, 'tis hot:there's that will sack a city.

Yes Hal. It's cooling down: there is something there that could sack a city.

[The Prince draws out a bottle of sack.]

PRINCE.
What, is't a time to jest and dally now?

What, is this a time for silly jokes?

[Throws it at him, and exit.]

FAL.
Well, if Percy be alive, I'll pierce him. If he do come in my
way, so; if he do not, if I come in his willingly, let him make
a carbonado of me. I like not such grinning honour as Sir
Walter hath:give me life; which if I can save, so; if not,
honour comes unlooked for, and there's an end.

Well, if Percy is alive, I'll stab him. If he comes in my
way, good; if he doesn't, I'll willingly come in his, and he can
make mincemeat of me. I don't like the sort of honour that Sir
Walter has: give me life; if I can save it, good; if not,
honour will come without me looking for it, that's all there is to it.

[Exit.]

Scene IV. Another Part of the Field.

[Alarums. Excursions. Enter King Henry, Prince Henry, Lancaster, and Westmoreland.]

KING.
I pr'ythee,
Harry, withdraw thyself; thou bleedest too much.--
Lord John of Lancaster, go you unto him.

Please, Harry,
retire; you are bleeding too much.
Lord John of Lancaster, you help him.

LAN.
Not I, my lord, unless I did bleed too.

Not me, my lord, unless I am bleeding too.

PRINCE.
I do beseech your Majesty, make up,
Lest your retirement do amaze your friends.

I beg your Majesty, go to the front,
so your retreat doesn't worry your friends.

KING.
I will do so.--
My Lord of Westmoreland, lead him to his tent.

I will do so.
My Lord of Westmorland, take him to his tent.

WEST.
Come, my lord, I'll lead you to your tent.

Come, my lord, I'll take you to your tent.

PRINCE.
Lead me, my lord?I do not need your help:

And God forbid, a shallow scratch should drive
The Prince of Wales from such a field as this,
Where stain'd nobility lies trodden on,
And rebels' arms triumph in massacres!

Take me, my lord? I do not need your help:
and God forbid that a little scratch would drive
the Prince of Wales from a battlefield like this,
where nobility has been insulted and trodden on,
and the rebels are triumphing in a massacre!

LAN.
We breathe too long:--come, cousin Westmoreland,
Our duty this way lies; for God's sake, come.

We have been talking too long: come, cousin Westmoreland,
this is where our duty lies; for God's sake, come.

[Exeunt Lancaster and Westmoreland.]

PRINCE.
By Heaven, thou hast deceived me, Lancaster;
I did not think thee lord of such a spirit:
Before, I loved thee as a brother, John;
But now I do respect thee as my soul.

By heaven, you have deceived me, Lancaster;
I did not think you were a Lord of such spirit:
before, I loved you as a brother, John;
but now I respect you as my equal.

KING.
I saw him hold Lord Percy at the point
With lustier maintenance than I did look for
Of such an ungrown warrior.

I saw him fighting Lord Percy with his sword
with more fortitude than I expected
from such a young soldier.

PRINCE.
O, this boy
Lends mettle to us all!

Oh, this boy
puts spirit in us all!

[Exit.]

[Alarums. Enter Douglas.]

DOUG.
Another king! they grow like Hydra's heads:
I am the Douglas, fatal to all those
That wear those colours on them.--What art thou,
That counterfeit'st the person of a king?

Another king! They grow like the heads of a Hydra–
I am Douglas, fatal to all those
who wear the uniform. Who are you,
who imitates the King?

KING.
The King himself; who, Douglas, grieves at heart
So many of his shadows thou hast met,
And not the very King. I have two boys
Seek Percy and thyself about the field:
But, seeing thou fall'st on me so luckily,
I will assay thee; so, defend thyself.

I am the King himself; and Douglas, I am very sorry
that you have met so many of my imitators,
and not the true king. I have two boys
who are looking for you and Percy on the battlefield:
but, as you have so fortunately found me,
I'll put you to the test; so, defend yourself.

DOUG.
I fear thou art another counterfeit;
And yet, in faith, thou bear'st thee like a king:
But mine I'm sure thou art, whoe'er thou be,
And thus I win thee.

I fear you're another imposter;
and yet, I swear, you carry yourself like a king:
but whoever you are, I'm sure you're mine,
and so I will finish you.

[They fight; the King being in danger, re-enter Prince Henry.]

PRINCE.
Hold up thy head, vile Scot, or thou art like
Never to hold it up again! the spirits
Of valiant Shirley, Stafford, Blunt are in my arms:
It is the Prince of Wales that threatens thee;
Who never promiseth but he means to pay.--

[They fight:Douglas flies.]

Cheerly, my lord:how fares your Grace?
Sir Nicholas Gawsey hath for succour sent,
And so hath Clifton:I'll to Clifton straight.

Lift up your head, vile Scot, or you may
never hold it up again! The ghosts
of brave Shirley, Stafford and Blunt strengthened me:
it is the Prince of Wales who threatens you;
who never makes threats without backing them up.

Hello, my lord: how is your Grace doing?
Sir Nicholas Gawsey has called for assistance,
and so has Clifton: I'll go straight to Clifton.

KING.
Stay, and breathe awhile:
Thou hast redeem'd thy lost opinion;
And show'd thou makest some tender of my life,
In this fair rescue thou hast brought to me.

Wait, and catch your breath:
you have won back my good opinion of you;
and showed that you care about my life,
by undertaking this good rescue.

PRINCE.
O God, they did me too much injury
That ever said I hearken'd for your death!
If it were so, I might have let alone
Th' insulting hand of Douglas over you,
Which would have been as speedy in your end
As all the poisonous potions in the world,
And saved the treacherous labour of your son.

200

*Oh God, anyone who said I yearned for your death
was doing me an injustice!
If that were the case, I could have let
the haughty hand of Douglas remain over you,
which would have given you as quick a death
as all the poisons in the world,
and saved your son having to commit any treachery.*

KING.
Make up to Clifton:I'll to Sir Nicholas Gawsey.

You go to Clifton: I'll go to Sir Nicholas Gawsey.

[Exit.]

[Enter Hotspur.]

HOT.
If I mistake not, thou art Harry Monmouth.

If I'm not mistaken, you are Harry Monmouth.

PRINCE.
Thou speak'st as if I would deny my name.

You speak as if I would deny it.

HOT.
My name is Harry Percy.

My name is Harry Percy.

PRINCE.
Why, then I see
A very valiant rebel of the name.
I am the Prince of Wales; and think not, Percy,
To share with me in glory any more:
Two stars keep not their motion in one sphere;
Nor can one England brook a double reign,
Of Harry Percy and the Prince of Wales.

*Well then, I see
a very brave rebel of that name.*

I am the Prince of Wales; and do not think, Percy,
that you can be equal with me in glory any more:
two stars cannot share the same orbit;
and England cannot be ruled by both
Harry Percy and the Prince of Wales.

HOT.
Nor shall it, Harry; for the hour is come
To end the one of us; and would to God
Thy name in arms were now as great as mine!

And it shall not be, Harry; for the time has come
for one of us to die; and I wish to God
that your reputation as a soldier was as great as mine!

PRINCE.
I'll make it greater ere I part from thee;
And all the budding honours on thy crest
I'll crop, to make a garland for my head.

I'll make it greater before I leave you;
and I'll take all those feathers of your helmet
to make a garland for my head.

HOT.
I can no longer brook thy vanities.

I shan't tolerate your vanity any longer.

[They fight.]

[Enter Falstaff.]

FAL.
Well said, Hal! to it, Hal! Nay, you shall find no boy's
play here, I can tell you.

Well said, Hal! Go to it, Hal! No, you will not find any
schoolboy fighting here, I can tell you.

[Re-enter Douglas; he fights with Falstaff, who falls down as if
he were dead, and exit Douglas. Hotspure is wounded, and falls.]

HOT.

O Harry, thou hast robb'd me of my youth!
I better brook the loss of brittle life
Than those proud titles thou hast won of me;
They wound my thoughts worse than thy sword my flesh:
But thoughts the slave of life, and life Time's fool,
And Time, that takes survey of all the world,
Must have a stop. O, I could prophesy,
But that the earthy and cold hand of death
Lies on my tongue:no, Percy, thou art dust,
And food for--

O Harry, you have stolen my youth away!
I don't mind losing my fragile life
as much as losing those proud titles you have won from me;
that hurts my thoughts more than your sword hurts my flesh:
but thought is the slave of life, and life isthe fool of time,
and time, that controls the whole world,
must come to an end. O, I could make predictions,
but the earthy cold hand of death
has taken my tongue: no, Percy, you are dust,
and food for–

[Dies.]

PRINCE.
For worms, brave Percy:fare thee well, great heart!
Ill-weaved ambition, how much art thou shrunk!
When that this body did contain a spirit,
A kingdom for it was too small a bound;
But now two paces of the vilest earth
Is room enough. This earth that bears thee dead
Bears not alive so stout a gentleman.
If thou wert sensible of courtesy,
I should not make so dear a show of zeal:
But let my favours hide thy mangled face;
And, even in thy behalf, I'll thank myself
For doing these fair rites of tenderness.
Adieu, and take thy praise with thee to Heaven!
Thy ignominy sleep with thee in the grave,
But not remember'd in thy epitaph!--

[Sees Falstaff on the ground.]

What, old acquaintance? could not all this flesh

Keep in a little life? Poor Jack, farewell!
I could have better spared a better man:
O, I should have a heavy miss of thee,
If I were much in love with vanity!
Death hath not struck so fat a deer to-day,
Though many dearer, in this bloody fray.
Embowell'd will I see thee by-and-by:
Till then in blood by noble Percy lie.

For worms, brave Percy: farewell, great heart!
Ill-conceived ambition, how you have shrunk!
when this body contained a spirit,
a kingdom was not big enough for it;
but now a couple of yards of low earth
is room enough.The earth that supports you dead
does not support a greater living man.
If you could hear what I'm saying,
I wouldn't be so polite about you:
but let my banner hide your mangled face;
and I'll thank myself on your behalf
for conducting these gentle last rites.
Goodbye, and take your fame with you to Heaven!
May your bad deeds stay in your grave,
and not be the way you are remembered!

What, my old friend?Couldn't all this flesh
retain a little life?Poor Jack, farewell!
I could have better spared a better man:
Oh, I would miss you greatly,
if I was in love with frivolity!
Death didn't hit a fatter target today,
though many better, in this bloody battle.
I'll see that you are buried soon:
until then lie in your blood next to noble Percy.

[Exit.]

FAL.
[Rising.] Embowell'd! if thou embowel me to-day, I'll give you leave
to powder me and eat me too to-morrow. 'Sblood, 'twas time to
counterfeit, or that hot termagant Scot had paid me scot and lot too.
Counterfeit! I lie; I am no counterfeit:to die, is to be a
counterfeit; for he is but the counterfeit of a man who hath not the
life of a man:but to counterfeit dying, when a man thereby liveth,

is to be no counterfeit, but the true and perfect image of life indeed.
The better part of valour is discretion; in the which better part I
have saved my life.--
Zwounds, I am afraid of this gunpowder Percy, though he be dead:how,
if he should counterfeit too, and rise? by my faith, I am afraid he
would prove the better counterfeit. Therefore I'll make him sure; yea,
and I'll swear I kill'd him. Why may not he rise as well as I?
Nothing confutes me but eyes, and nobody sees me. Therefore,
sirrah, with a new wound in your thigh, come you along with me.

*Buried! If you bury me today, I'll give you permission
to pickle me and eat me tomorrow. By God, it was a time
to fake it, or that passionate quarrelling Scot would have finished me off.
Fake! I'm lying; I am not a fake: to die, is to be a
fake; for if you don't have the life of a man then you are just the imitation
of one: but to fake dying, in order to keep a man alive,
that is not faking, but the perfection of life.
The best part of valour is discretion; and using that better part I
have saved my life–*

*By God, I am afraid of this fiery Percy, although he is dead:
what if he is faking to, and gets up? By God, I am afraid he
would be a better faker. So I'll make sure of him; yes,
and I'll swear that I killed him. Why shouldn't he get up the same as I did?
Nobody could contradict me except an eyewitness, and there's nobody here. Therefore, Sir, with a
new wound in your thigh, you come along with me.*

[Takes Hotspur on his hack.]

[Re-enter Prince Henry and Lancaster.]

PRINCE.
Come, brother John; full bravely hast thou flesh'd
Thy maiden sword.

*Come, brother John; you have done a good job
with your virgin sword.*

LAN.
But, soft! whom have we here?
Did you not tell me this fat man was dead?

*But wait! What's this?
Didn't you tell me this fat man was dead?*

PRINCE.

I did; I saw him dead, breathless and bleeding
Upon the ground.--
Art thou alive? or is it fantasy
That plays upon our eyesight? I pr'ythee, speak;
We will not trust our eyes without our ears.
Thou art not what thou seem'st.

I did; I saw him dead, breathless and bleeding
on the ground.
Are you alive? Or is it
a trick of the light? I beg you, speak;
we won't trust our eyes without our ears.
You are not what you seem.

FAL.

No, that's certain; I am not a double man:but if I be not
Jack Falstaff, then am I a Jack. There is Percy![Throwing the
body down.] if your father will do me any honour, so; if not, let
him kill the next Percy himself. I look to be either earl or
duke, I can assure you.

No, that's certain; I am not an apparition: but if I am not
Jack Falstaff, then I am a knave: there is Percy!
If your father wants to honour me for it, good; if not,
he can kill the next Percy himself. I can tell you I think I should be
either an earl or Duke.

PRINCE.

Why, Percy I kill'd myself, and saw thee dead.

Why, I killed Percy myself, and saw you dead.

FAL.

Didst thou?-- Lord, Lord, how this world is given to lying!--
I grant you I was down and out of breath; and so was he:but
we rose both at an instant, and fought a long hour by Shrewsbury
clock. If I may be believed, so; if not, let them that should
reward valour bear the sin upon their own heads. I'll take it upon
my death, I gave him this wound in the thigh:if the man were
alive, and would deny it, zwounds, I would make him eat a piece of
my sword.

Did you? Lord, Lord, how many liars there are in this world!
I admit I was down and out of breath; and so was he: but
we both rose at the same time, and fought for a long hour
by Shrewsbury clock. If you will believe me, good; if not, let those
who should reward bravery carry the sin on their heads. I swear
on my life, I gave him this wound in the thigh: if there is any man
alive who wants to deny it, by God, I will make him eat some of
my sword.

LAN.
This is the strangest tale that ever I heard.

This is the strangest tale I ever heard.

PRINCE.
This is the strangest fellow, brother John.--
Come, bring your luggage nobly on your back:
For my part, if a lie may do thee grace,
I'll gild it with the happiest terms I have.--

This is the strangest fellow, brother John.
Come, carry your luggage nobly on your back:
as for me, if a lie will do you good,
I'll help it along as best I can–

[A retreat is sounded.]

The trumpet sounds retreat; the day is ours.
Come, brother, let's to th' highest of the field,
To see what friends are living, who are dead.

The trumpet sounds the retreat; we have won.
Come, brother, let's go to the highest point of the battlefield,
to see what friends are alive, and who has died.

[Exeunt Prince Henry and Lancaster.]

FAL.
I'll follow, as they say, for reward. He that rewards me, God
reward him! If I do grow great, I'll grow less; for I'll purge,
and leave sack, and live cleanly as a nobleman should do.

I'll follow, as they say, for reward. Whoever rewards me, may
God reward him! If I become great, I shall shrink; for I will starve myself,

and leave off drinking, and live a clean life as a nobleman should.

[Exit, bearing off the body.]

Scene V. Another Part of the Field.

[The trumpets sound. Enter King Henry, Prince Henry,
Lancaster, Westmoreland, and others, with Worcester and
Vernon prisoners.]

KING.
Thus ever did rebellion find rebuke.--
Ill-spirited Worcester! did not we send grace,
Pardon, and terms of love to all of you?
And wouldst thou turn our offers contrary?
Misuse the tenour of thy kinsman's trust?
Three knights upon our party slain to-day,
A noble earl, and many a creature else,
Had been alive this hour,
If, like a Christian, thou hadst truly borne
Betwixt our armies true intelligence.

And so rebellions have always failed.
Ill spirited Worcester! Didn't we offer forgiveness,
pardon, and love to all of you?
And you had to turn our offers down?
You abused the trust your kinsman placed in you.
Three knights from our army were killed today,
a noble Earl, and many other men,
who would have been alive now,
if you had behaved like a Christian and
truthfully carried the messages between our armies.

WOR.
What I have done my safety urged me to;
And I embrace this fortune patiently,
Since not to be avoided it fails on me.

I did what I had to for my own safety;
and I stoically accept my fate,
since it is unavoidable.

KING.
Bear Worcester to the death, and Vernon too:

Other offenders we will pause upon.--

[Exeunt Worcester and Vernon, guarded.]

How goes the field?

Take Worcester to be executed, and Vernon too:
we will suspend sentence on the other offenders–
how is the battle?

PRINCE.
The noble Scot, Lord Douglas, when he saw
The fortune of the day quite turn'd from him,
The noble Percy slain, and all his men
Upon the foot of fear, fled with the rest;
And, falling from a hill, he was so bruised
That the pursuers took him. At my tent
The Douglas is:and I beseech your Grace
I may dispose of him.

The noble Scot, Lord Douglas, when he saw
that the tide had quite turned against him,
with the noble Percy slain, and all his men
running in fear, he ran with the rest;
and, falling down a hill, he was so injured
that the pursuers captured him. The Douglas
is in my tent: and I beg your grace
that I be allowed to dispose of him.

KING.
With all my heart.

Of course.

PRINCE.
Then, brother John of Lancaster, to you
This honourable bounty shall belong:
Go to the Douglas, and deliver him
Up to his pleasure, ransomless and free:
His valour, shown upon our crests to-day,
Hath taught us how to cherish such high deeds
Even in the bosom of our adversaries.

Then, brother John of Lancaster, you

shall have this honourable task:
go to the Douglas, and let him
go where he wants, free without ransom:
his bravery, which you can see from the dents in my helmet,
has taught me how to value such great deeds,
even when they are done by our enemies.

KING.
Then this remains, that we divide our power.--
You, son John, and my cousin Westmoreland,
Towards York shall bend you with your dearest speed,
To meet Northumberland and the prelate Scroop,
Who, as we hear, are busily in arms:
Myself,--and you, son Harry,--will towards Wales,
To fight with Glendower and the Earl of March.
Rebellion in this land shall lose his sway,
Meeting the check of such another day;
And since this business so fair is done,
Let us not leave till all our own be won.

Then all that remains is to divide our forces.
You, my son John, and my cousin Westmoreland,
shall go to York as fast as you can,
to fight Northumberland and the Bishop Scroop,
who, we hear, are busy arming themselves:
myself–and you, son Harry–will go towards Wales,
to fight with Glendower and the Earl of March.
If the rebellion has to face another day
like this one it will lose its power;
as we've had such a good result here,
let's not stop until we have triumphed over all.

[Exeunt.]

The End

Printed in Great Britain
by Amazon.co.uk, Ltd.,
Marston Gate.